Simone Jones is a parent of two young men now in their twenties. Currently, an Educational Psychologist and recently a yoga teacher, she is also a qualified Nursery Nurse, Montessori teacher and HighScope Practitioner, having worked in preschools supporting children under five years for over ten years previous to her psychology career. Since her experience of brain injury, she is passionate about sharing her journey in support of others and in raising awareness of acquired brain injury.

Rupture Repair

How I Chose to Be Happy:
Life After a Brain Injury

Simone Jones

Rupture Repair

How I Chose to Be Happy: Life After a Brain Injury

Vanguard Press

VANGUARD PAPERBACK

© Copyright 2024
Simone Jones

A CIP catalogue record for this title is
available from the British Library.

ISBN 978 1 80016 967 8

Vanguard Press is an imprint of
Pegasus Elliot Mackenzie Publishers Ltd.
www.pegasuspublishers.com

First Published in 2024

Vanguard Press
Sheraton House Castle Park
Cambridge England

Printed & Bound in Great Britain

To my two young men, Dylan and Owen, who have gifted me with so much love and learning in my life. To my ex-husband, Paul, for his support and dedication to me in my immediate need, in my sickness, and in my health in our younger years.

To my sons, my parents, family and friends, for all the support along my recovery journey. I am forever grateful.

Contents

Chapter One

Pumped Up

If you do not give time to your wellness, you will be forced to give time to your illness. — Joyce Sunada, wellness coach, of joyfulendeavours.com

Now read that again! "If you do not give time to your wellness, you will be forced to give time to your illness." That is a statement that resonates strongly with me. It gives me shivers, in fact, mainly because I know it to be true and I have learned it the hard way.

It was a cold December Friday morning, and I woke with contentment due to it being my day off. I had some annual leave from work left that I hadn't taken which needed to be used up by the end of the year. If you don't use it, you'll lose it, sort of thing. I had decided, instead of losing it, I would take Fridays off in the last couple of weeks in the run-up to Christmas. With the work Christmas party coming up and some other gatherings planned, I had several beauty appointments booked in over the coming week. This morning, I had a pedicure appointment. I was looking forward to the 'me' time, time to close my eyes, relax and enjoy the downtime. Work had been hectic this week. This was a well-deserved treat which was becoming a bit of a habit! Being a tomboy in middle childhood, I was never really a girly girl, into hair, nails, and make-up. In the past, I had always tended to get my hair cut for functional reasons rather than the enjoyment of the act itself. I didn't bother with my nails either. I didn't enjoy the hassle of salons and found small talk uncomfortable. When my children were young, it just didn't seem a priority. I also did not like to wear dresses. It had always annoyed me that there was an expectation for females to wear dresses, mainly in relation to school uniforms, among other times. I believed I was demonstrating my protest by dressing in tracksuits and jeans mainly. "I don't wear dresses" or "this is a long top" often being my tagline. But I had started to soften in my maturing years and had worn dresses more often recently, becoming more confident to have my legs on view. I had also started to find getting my nails done more relaxing than I ever had before. Being familiar with the salon and going to the same nail technician, Connie, every time has helped with that. I mostly go for a French polish or a neutral tone on my fingernails with a pop of colour around festive times or for holidays.

But today, I was not going to my usual salon. I had booked into a 'pop-up' salon in support of a local beauty college that set up the 'pop-up' salon at certain times of the year to give their students extra experience. In settling into my position in the chair, I decided on a deep red colour with one silver glittery toenail. Very festive and on-trend, I thought! The toenail colour was not too far off the colour already on my fingernails, which I had painted two weeks ago for my eldest son's twenty-first birthday party. I was planning to change my fingernail colour next week to something different for the work party. During my time at the pop-up salon, I could feel myself start to relax slightly, but because I was not in my usual salon, I was alert to the noises around me in this environment. I was also being nosy. I like to observe and people-watch. I found myself looking around the room at other students, wondering how they were feeling. I was definitely picking up on nervous tension. Not necessarily from the student I was assigned, she seemed quietly confident. But others in the room nervously moved items from one space to another or whispered questions to each other about what to do next or how they might manage their appointments. I found this mildly entertaining. Not out of any malice, but because I could relate to the feeling, particularly in learning something new or with new experiences. I was glad I was on the other side, enjoying the treatment. But at the same time, wanting to soothe their nerves for them, encouraging them to relax and enjoy the experience.

Delighted, with my nails painted, I headed home. There were household chores I wanted to do and I was booked into a gym class at five p.m. later in the day that I wanted to be organised for. I had lunch and pottered about with my chores. I was playing songs on my phone that I enjoyed singing to. I was also learning to sing a new song so I sang on repeat, driving my youngest son mad, indicated by the shouts of, "how much longer are you going to keep singing?" Listening with my earphones in and singing at the top of my voice, I'm sure it became tiresome!

Changing into my gym gear, I seemed to have difficulty deciding what to wear. I didn't usually falter too much when deciding what to wear to the gym. I wasn't someone who felt that I needed to dress up to go to the gym. In my head, the gym is where I go to exercise, which means being a sweaty mess! That is meant as no judgement. Just, for me, I didn't care much for eye make-up or lipstick as an everyday thing, so it just wouldn't make sense to me when planning to be sweaty during and after a session. I would be somebody who would have make-up rolling down their face in that case, so it wasn't really appealing to go to any effort. My hair is in a short bob, so I'm lucky to about manage to tie the top part with a hair bobbin, just to keep the hair out of my eyes. I chose a grey pair of leggings and a soft blue long-sleeve top. On reflection, I am not sure why I chose the long sleeve top. I think I had thought something about it being comfier, but I just shrugged off the indecision and gathered my towel, water bottle, phone, and jacket. Having listened to songs on my phone all afternoon, the phone battery was nearly empty. "Meh," I thought, "I won't need it during the class and I'm going home straight after, I'll charge it then." I was planning to get to the gym a little earlier than the class to put my phone, car keys and jacket in the locker. But with the delay in deciding what to wear and changing clothes, I was leaving myself no time to go to the dressing room. The entrance hall to Westpark gym has a set of approximately seven steps up to it between the main glass door and the second glass door to the reception. I took those steps in twos as I was attending a 'Body Pump' exercise class which was held in the studio room upstairs at the back, off the main gym floor. It required some individual equipment set-up. So, I went straight upstairs to the studio, bypassing the dressing room. The studio has floor-to-ceiling internal glass separating it from the main gym floor with a full glass door entrance. It also has floor-to-ceiling grey windows with grey windowsills at floor level looking out over the car park and a local park. I managed to pick my favourite spot, right by the window in the middle row. Although the view out of the window at this time of day was pitch black in the depths of winter, I still felt the comfort of having more space. Being in the middle row, I also felt somewhat hidden from the limelight of the front row. I placed my keys in my jacket pocket and placed my jacket on the windowsill. Tossing my phone on top of the jacket, on one percent battery, I wondered why I had bothered to bring it at all. I headed over to the opposite wall to gather my much-needed equipment for the class.

A Les Mills 'BODYPUMP ™' class is a full-body barbell class designed to burn calories, shape, and tone the entire body. It was one of my favourite classes to attend in the gym. I went about gathering my equipment quickly. I needed a step, a weight bar, and some varying weight plates. At least two trips to the weight rack are required. When I returned from the rack the second time with weight plates, I noticed I had picked up the same weight plates I already had the first time. Thinking that was a strange thing, I went back with the weight plates and got larger size weight plates, as I originally intended. I shrugged it off and thought I must be feeling tired. The class began with the instructor's booming voice over the mic to signify the start of the class. It was a high-tempo forty-five-minute class with music pumping, and I started strongly. I soon noticed I was a bit 'off,' wondering if I had eaten enough. Being a five p.m. class, it was too early to eat dinner, with enough time before the class. So, I had a light snack just over an hour ago. I also wondered if I was a little more tired than usual, but I kept going. One part of the class involves doing back squats, where the barbell rests on the shoulders at the base of the neck. It has a sequence, something like three normal back squats, three pulsing squats, where you stay lower, and three normal squats again. I had attended this class multiple times and was familiar with the sequence. But today, for some reason, I seemed to be out of sync with the rest of the group. Every time I was supposed to be pulsing, my body decided to pop back up again, so I was doing a full squat. It was like I knew what I needed to do in my head but automatically my body just kept popping back up, like some delayed reaction. I was slightly embarrassed but sort of laughed it off, saying to myself, "why am I doing this?"

The exercise quickly changed to the chest press. Lying with my back on the step, my knees bent and two feet on the floor, the expectation was to hold a weight plate on my chest and engage the sequence: straight up from the chest, over the head, back to above the chest and back down on the chest. This is a reasonably easy movement, but I felt I became slightly unsure of the sequence and looked to the instructor. This meant keeping my body in the same position but turning my head to the left to see the instructor. I noticed a pain in my head on the left side when I did this. I thought perhaps my hair bobbin was catching and pressing on the step. Then I thought I must have tied my hair bobbin too tight today somehow. As I moved the plate from above my chest to over my head, I noticed the plate twisted to the side, like steering a car steering wheel. This happened every time I looked to the instructor but stopped when I looked directly at the plate. I thought, "This is weird, what is up with me today?" Then we changed exercise again to kneeling at the side of the step doing one-arm rows with the weight plate. I seemed to be transitioning slower to each exercise and a little hesitant, with the need to check with the instructor, to follow her guidance. This is one hundred percent unusual for me. I was slower than usual, but not by much. Most likely not noticeable to others, but I could feel it. In changing exercise again to a press-up on the step, I felt a little queasy after the first two. It rushed over me like a wave and I wondered how I was going to get up to leave. I really did not want to vomit there and then in the class. I had to leave a different class earlier in the week for feeling queasy, breathless, and faint. I had managed to leave, step outside the class to gather myself and go again after a minute's rest. But this felt different somehow like I knew I wouldn't make it to the door. "Maybe it will pass, maybe just keep on going," I said to myself. In trying the press-up again, I stopped, kneeling in front of the step. I felt the room spin slightly. Suddenly, I felt an immense thunderclap pain across the left side of my head. I put my hand up to the side of my head. I had a flash thought, "is this that 'thing' that person had?" I couldn't figure out what to do, so thought, "just push through, do another press up and see how you feel."

Chapter Two

Floored

"Simone, Simone, do you know where you are?" a voice was saying in the distance. Of course, I knew where I was! "I'm in bed having a lovely sleep," I thought to myself. That lovely sleep where you are lying on the comfiest pillows in the world, snuggled in the comfiest duvet in the world with beautiful warm sunshine beaming through the curtains, heating the whole room. That floaty, light feeling. It was such a peaceful morning and such a lovely sleep I was having. Rousing gently, "Please, don't disturb me, this is blissful," I said inside my head.

"Simone, my name is Stephen. You are in the gym, you've collapsed and have been out for six minutes, an ambulance is on the way." Now the words, ambulance is on the way, woke me from that blissful slumber. How was I in the gym? That made no sense. I was in my comfy bed... was I not?

Coming to, and with half-opened eyes, I noticed that it wasn't sunlight beaming in but the bright lights of the studio. Closing my eyes again to block out the sheer intensity of the glow and in the hope this vertigo feeling that suddenly began would dissipate. "How am I on the floor?" and "why do I need an ambulance?" I thought. "I must have just fainted. I probably didn't eat enough of a snack beforehand. Sure, I'll just get up in a second when I get my bearings and the room stops spinning." I paused for thought. "Maybe I was having a 'hypo'," I said to myself. I had been placed on medication earlier in the summer months for concerns related to possible insulin resistance. I had found sometimes when I came back from the gym in the summer months that I needed to lie down. I had gotten a vertigo feeling, my lips tingled, and I felt disorientated or confused. If someone asked me something or placed a higher cognitive demand on me, I mostly needed extra time to answer or to rest. A short rest and a piece of chocolate or something sugary usually sorted me. This felt a little like those times. "So, it must be just that," I thought, even though I had stopped taking the medication months ago.

Because the light was burning my eyes, I kept them closed, only opening them slightly. Seeing my right arm outstretched in front of me was about as much as I could see. I got a sense that the voice of 'Stephen' was beside me or above me, but close by. I had no idea where I was in the room and I had no sense of the floor below me or what I was lying on. It felt like I was lying on air. I couldn't recall the gym floor to even get a sense of what the floor covering was. Then came another male voice. He was talking on the phone on and off and he introduced himself as Dave. He reported that I had been working hard, "giving it loads" during the class.

I answered, "No, I wasn't." He laughed nervously. I felt confused. I wasn't sure why he was saying that or laughing. I knew myself I did not perform well in the class, so I was just being honest. Stephen asked me some questions about my medical history. I found I could answer 'yes' and 'no' and some one-word answers. When he asked me if I had anything else in my medical history, I tried to communicate about possibly being insulin resistant, but I found I couldn't remember those words. I was trying to remember the word 'hypo,' but I couldn't think of that either. Even the word diabetes (which I knew was not what I had) escaped me. I was really tired with just trying to remember what the words were.

In attempting to move, I found that I couldn't lift my head off the floor. I screamed, "my head!" in pain and confusion as to what was going on. My hands went up to my head to try to stop this burning, gnawing pain. I was in immense pain with a strange painful sensation rolling around my head. "What is that?" I wondered. The pain circulated.

"Ow, ow, ow, my head," I said. I've never experienced pain like it and I have given birth twice. I can only describe the sensation as if my head was like a bowling ball with liquid rolling around in it. I sighed and my body went limp.

I could hear Stephen's voice say, "She's gone again." "What did he mean gone again? I wasn't gone anywhere.

I was still here and I can hear everything you are saying. This is weird," I thought. "I should be more alert and I should be able to get up off the floor by now. Why does my head hurt?" I wondered why my head hurt so much with a 'hypo.'

I saw my phone slide along the floor in front of my face. Dave asked if I could put in my PIN code. My PIN code came to my mind, but I had no idea what Dave wanted me to do with the phone. So, I just stared at it. The phone was removed, and I heard him say, "it's on one percent anyway." Stephen's voice came closer to me and he asked if there was anyone he could contact while we waited on the ambulance. I did not respond.

"Is there anyone that you need, Simone," the gentle voice said again.

With a deep intake of breath, "I need Paul," I mumbled.

Here comes that horrendous pain again. I put my hands up to my head, screaming. I was cursing also, "my fucking head, my fucking head." At this point, I started pulling my hair. I also began banging my foot off the ground, in some way to shift the focus from the pain. Again, I sighed as if in exhaustion and my body went limp.

"She's gone again," I heard. I could hear Stephen and Dave talking. I heard Stephen ask where the ambulance was. I heard Stephen say he was supposed to be travelling up to Belfast for a Christmas party that evening and he had friends waiting for him in the car.

"Go if you need to go," Dave said.

"No, I'll wait on the ambulance," said Stephen. They talked back and forth about what was keeping the ambulance, wondering what was going on and how long it would be.

Another round of this dreadful pain. I couldn't take much more of it. I began pounding my foot off the ground rhythmically, there was something almost soothing in it. It was distracting from the pain in my head slightly. Stephen's hand on my head, stopping me from pulling my hair out was also somewhat soothing. Still, the pain went around and around. I tried moving my other leg and found nothing was happening.

Panicked, I murmured, "I can't move my leg."

Dave joked, "You can, sure you're moving it now!"

"No, my other leg," I said. Something in Dave's voice worried me.

Stephen's soft voice said, "It's okay." I started to think I was in trouble. I knew I couldn't find the words I needed. I knew I couldn't move one of my legs. I just couldn't be sure if it were my right or my left one. I hadn't known what to do with my phone. I'm not able to lift my head off the floor. The light is burning my eyes and I have no sense of where I am in space. I should be able to get up by now. And why is my head in so much pain? I knew this was serious. I knew I had to get to hospital. I knew I had to hang on, I knew I had to survive.

"Where's the ambulance?" I whispered.

Stephen replied, "It's on the way, it's just stuck in traffic."

"Dylan, what are you doing here?" said Dave.

I could hear Dylan's voice draw near and say, "That's my mam. Why is she still here?" Dylan came over and said, "Her arm has gone blue and she's cold." I opened my eyes ajar. My hair was covering the glare of the lights and I could see my outstretched arm was indeed a blue tinge. He placed my jacket on the top half of my body. I could hear them chatting but I was unsure where in the room they were. I knew Stephen was right beside me, like a warm energy. I kept telling myself, "Hold on for the ambulance, you just need to get to the hospital."

The wait was agonising. Suddenly, there was movement, like waves rolling underneath me with every thud of heavy boots. Different voices, new voices were heard now, questioning. Something inside said to shift off my right arm. I tried to move, to turn myself over, and the room spun ferociously. Lying on my back, exhausted, I turned my head to the left. I vomited and saw a white towel pushed under my head. Resting my head on it, my body was now on the opposite side, but my arm flopped behind me. I felt very alone. I couldn't hear Stephen's gentle voice any more. Just serious voices, booming loudly. There was a comment about my arm being blue. I felt a sharp pinch at the back of my upper right arm and I cried out. Why were they hurting me? I was already in enough pain. Again, waves of movement and murmuring. I was now rolled onto my back. The light burned through the slits of my eyes and I could hear a count of three. "One, two, three," and I was lifted off the floor and placed onto an emergency gurney chair.

"My neck, my neck," I screamed as the same excruciating pain from my head moved down to my neck. I could not support my head in the chair. My head rolled back, hanging off the back of the chair but at least it was in the least painful position. I knew I was being brought out of the gym as I could see the tiled roof above me, but I was unable to focus or get a sense of where I was in the gym; I could just feel the movement. My body slumped in the chair, unable to control my posture. My hands hung limply from my wrists in front of me. Descending in the open wheelchair lift, as Dylan walked down the entrance steps, our eyes locked. He looked ashen-faced. I tried to move my arm out to him to connect with him, but my body wouldn't respond. I tried to speak to him to tell him I was going to be okay, but nothing would come out of my mouth. I couldn't even get my lips to move or my mouth to open. I was hoping he could understand what I was saying with my eyes. This is horrific, I felt. "Is this what locked-in syndrome feels like?" I thought.

Chapter Three

Holding On

In the ambulance, I could hear the paramedic ask Dylan if I had gone unconscious at any time. Dylan replied that he didn't think so. I wondered why the paramedic hadn't asked Stephen for those details as he had been with me all the way through and could have informed him. Feeling it was vital that the paramedic have the correct answer, I propped myself up with all I could muster, with my eyes closed, and blurted out Stephen's earlier words.

"I was out for six minutes," I said and slumped back down with a sigh.

Next, I was in the hospital. I was lying on my right side again and I remember the doctor leaning in close, asking me questions. He asked if I could be pregnant.

"No," I replied confidently. He asked me the dates of my last menstrual cycle. "Last month," I muttered, using all my strength. It had fallen on the same day of the month in both October and November.

"What date?" he asked. I gave him the date saying, "13th October."

"October?" the Doctor replied inquisitively. "But that's not last month," he said. The only month that would come to mind was October. So, if last month wasn't October, then I didn't have an answer. He asked again. I couldn't even explain what I was thinking. I opened my mouth but only a sigh would come out. Thinking and speaking took a lot of energy.

I couldn't get a sense of where I was. In one way, I knew I was in hospital. But in another way, I couldn't tell. I had no sense of any walls, ceilings, or floors. I knew I was lying down but had no sense of what I was lying on. Voices seemed to float around the atmosphere. Two nurses on either side of me called my name.

One said, "Come on, Simone, you have to help get undressed." I was pulled to sitting from behind my shoulder blades. I had no control over my body. In the split second, I was upright, I looked down at my clothes. I had no idea how they would come off. Like a ragdoll, I flopped back down onto the bed. I heard one nurse tut loudly. Did they not realise I was very unwell? If I could have helped, I would have. I wasn't drunk and hadn't taken some illegal substance. But my body was acting as if I had.

I was on the move again. Once again, I was just getting the sensation in my body that I was moving. I was transferred onto something, I had no idea what, but it was cold. I could feel extreme cold go through my body and I began to shake. In the background, I could hear my parents and my husband talking. I couldn't figure out where they were. It seemed their voices came from the top of my head, but further back from my head, with the sound drifting as if it floated down a long corridor. But not a corridor of walls. Everything seemed like it was energy, nothing was solid. It just flowed, infinitely. Like it may in another dimension.

I could hear my mother crying. I heard the doctor apologise and confirm that I had had a "bleed to the brain," and I needed to be transferred to Beaumont Hospital, the National Centre for Neurosurgery, as soon as possible for surgery. I wasn't shocked. I was more relieved than anything else. It was as if I had known hours ago. From my profession and understanding of the brain, I knew I was in trouble when I was lying on that gym floor. I knew I had to survive until I got from the gym to the hospital. Now, again, I knew I had to survive the next bit and I knew I would be okay once I got to the other hospital.

"Come on, Simone, you need to take this," came a harsh-sounding voice. Well, that was how I interpreted it. Was she the one from earlier, trying to get me to undress? I wondered. I was propped up slightly and I could feel something against my lips. I pursed my lips tightly shut. What was that 'mean woman' trying to give me? I don't like to take medication at the best of times. I can be suspicious of what is in medication and how it alters the body. I hadn't even ever taken a sleeping tablet for fear of what it might do. I prefer feeling in control and don't like the possible sensation or even grogginess medication could potentially induce. "Come on, Simone, you need to take this," said the familiar and gentle voice of my dad into my ear. I groaned. "It's to help you get better, come on, take it, for me," he said. I relaxed and took the medication just as he asked.

The pain in my head never went away and I lay still. I could hear women chatting and laughing in good festive spirits. It felt like I was at a pub and the women were at the bar ordering drinks while I was hiding under a pub table, extremely drunk, hovering into a hangover with a pounding headache. The noise felt like a gnawing woodpecker that would not stop.

"Shhh," I managed to say. My husband asked what was up and I said the noise was too loud.

I could hear him say, "Any chance of keeping the noise down slightly, she's really unwell?" As if the next-door neighbours were having a party and he was asking them to lower the music. He said that the nurse's station was right outside and there were a couple of nurses gathered. The noise eased and I appreciated that.

I felt cold, the worst cold feeling I could imagine. I was shivering uncontrollably. I had no energy. I felt like I was dying. It was at that moment that I had a feeling of extreme calm. It wasn't that I had felt panicked or scared before. I had been in survival mode. But this feeling was not like before. Earlier, the feeling of energy corridor, another dimension, felt separate to me. Like I was lying at the top of the corridor, looking down it, watching the energy pass by. This time, it was a feeling like my body was the energy and could slip into and join the other energy and float down this infinite serene energy corridor.

A voice calmly said, "You can let go, if that is what you would like."

"It's okay to go now…" I wasn't scared to go. In fact, it was so peaceful, it was encouraging to go.

Chapter Four

Childhood Dreams

When you hear the word 'wellness,' what does that mean to you? When I think about wellness, it includes practising healthy habits to support a healthy body and a healthy mind. In my instance, if we rewind twelve months prior to collapsing at the gym, to all on the outside looking in, I was a fit and healthy young woman. "How could she be lying in a hospital bed?" some said. Their perception or their version of me was what I wanted them to see: A woman interested in health and fitness, a wife, a mother of two children, a psychologist, a fun and social person. The happy-go-lucky kind. A woman putting herself out there and challenging herself. I was eating well, going to the gym often and connecting with family and friends. I was engaging in self-care practices and I was challenging myself also.

These challenges mainly related to unaccomplished goals that I had in my early life. I sang in the school choir as a child, as shy as I was, and had always wanted to join the local youth church choir when I became a teenager. Only to discover when I became of age, that I didn't think it was cool any more, and as I was rebelling against my religion, at that time, I'm sure I couldn't have joined anyway! Therefore, that goal was never achieved. I was the shy type and I found, as I grew into adolescence and on into adulthood, doing a 'party piece' even at a family gathering to be cringe-worthy. The only place singing had in my life was when my children were young and in my job as a preschool teacher. Even then, I stood back shyly as a colleague of mine, with an incredibly beautiful voice, rightly took centre stage.

But having just turned thirty-eight years of age and eager to act on my 'forty things to do before I turned forty' goal (forty before forty), I decided to take action on this closet singing. I researched local singing lessons and began a set of ten singing lessons. I was so nervous; no sound would come out of my mouth. Crippled with social awkwardness in front of one person, the singing teacher, how was I going to join a choir?

What I realised was that the uncomfortable, anxious feelings in my body were what I didn't like about singing. I loved to sing and could sing with ease when alone, with the ability to hit high notes. But put me in front of someone and ask me to sing, and all the feelings associated with social anxiety flood in: the sting of my cheeks burning with embarrassment with all eyes on me, the tension in my muscles as I stood rigid, the tightness in my jaw, the awkward moving of my hands. That churning sensation in my stomach, my heart beating fast, the noise of the heartbeat pulsating in my ear, the tightening of my chest, my breathing restricted and my throat closing over, with little room for air to get into breathe, never mind sing. All of that, plus my thoughts racing: "I don't like it," "I don't like this sensation," "She thinks you are rubbish (the singing teacher)," "She's wondering why you are here (the singing teacher)," "This is so embarrassing," "I can't breathe," "I need to leave," "I need to get out," "If you leave the feeling will go away," "The easier thing to do would be to avoid it," "Stop going to the lessons, I don't need this in my life," "I don't need to put myself out there," "I don't need to join a choir," "This is mad at your age." "You are not good enough to sing in a choral society," "Everyone will laugh at you anyway," "The Choirmaster will wonder what you are doing there."

The 'gremlin' inside my head said these things, repeatedly. The thoughts, coupled with the feelings, perpetuated cyclically. As soon as I would leave the lesson, the feelings dissipated and I felt good for having gotten through it. Back in the lesson the following week, the feelings would start again. Then, the 'gremlin' appears. As I learn some techniques and get an understanding of what is needed to breathe, to sing properly, I realised that I had to be relaxed to sing. There was no option but to 'show up' calm for me. Otherwise, there was no point in attending. The singing teacher's nod of reassurance as she played the piano alongside my singing and her kind words of encouragement and comment about my "chocolate tones" echoed in my head long after the lesson was over.

I found a way to stay calm and shut that gremlin up, and in the coming months, I overcame my nervousness and plucked up the courage to audition for my local choral society. On the night of the audition, walking up to the building, those anxious feelings returned, and the gremlin raised his ugly head again. I decided to take some breaths to manage my breathing and with positive self-talk: "You've got this," "You can do it," "You are a lovely singer," "Chocolate tones," "You are going to have so much fun singing in a group," "Remember the article you read on singing in a group and the positive outcomes it can have," "You would be an asset to any choir," "You will feel so free." The thoughts then became: "I've got this," "I can do this," "I am confident and brave," "I am a lovely singer," "I am going to enjoy this," "I feel free." And enjoy it I did! The choirmaster reported that I had a good vocal range. Having told her before the audition that I thought I was an alto, she reported that I was actually a soprano and a soprano one at that! She suggested I start at soprano two to build confidence first. I was ecstatic, delighted with life, on a natural high. I got such a boost. Weekly rehearsals of singing in a group felt fantastic, just as the article had suggested. I had only watched concerts in venues such as the National Concert Hall in Dublin, among others, but I was feeling really excited about getting to participate in a concert myself.

When I look back to childhood, imagination paired with no inhibitions (to a certain degree, mainly within the comfort of my own home) was a wonderful thing. I loved gymnastics and watching figure skating. I was flexible, being able to do the splits, handstands, and cartwheels, and with no fear of heights, I imagined I would be a great gymnast. When I watched figure skating, I could imagine myself being able to do all the moves. I would throw myself up onto the sofa trying out moves, and in my head, I was able for it! I could imagine wonderful things for myself.

Another childhood dream of mine was to become a professional footballer in the English Premiership League! I have memories of middle childhood; being a tomboy who enjoyed playing football with the lads. I had a bit of a chip on my shoulder about gender equality, but I didn't know it as that then. At first, the boys always picked me last to be on a team, but as my confidence grew and they saw how good at football I was, I began to be picked earlier than last and that was good enough for me. I loved sport. I loved any sport in which I could engage. It was what got me through my teenage years. The Spice Girls girl band were big at that time, and although I didn't like their music, I was referred to as 'Sporty Spice.'

As a female in the early 1990s in Ireland, my hopes for the dream of becoming an English Premiership footballer were cut short when I hit puberty and realised that women didn't play on the men's teams! In fact, there was not much room for women in football at that time. With many a remark of "Girls can't play football," "Girls don't play football," and "Girls don't know the offside rule." Nonetheless, I was determined to follow my passion and drive to be a footballer. I played for the school football team, my home football team, and I even attended trials for the Irish National Women's football team when I was sixteen-years-old.

I don't remember much about the trials that day. I think I have blocked a lot of it. But what I do remember is the disappointment was rife. I didn't perform. I was unwell with a chest infection. I was on an antibiotic and Ventolin, a drug for the relief of bronchial asthma, to open the airways. On reflection, the stress, excitement, and nervousness of the pending day most likely manifested in a sickness, a somatic complaint presenting in a chest infection. As a result, I was not feeling great. I had asthma all my life. I never allowed asthma to get in my way and I was determined not to let it get in my way that day. Instead, something else got in the way. My shyness and social anxiety. Being confident and competent on my home team was one thing, but take me out of my comfort zone and the shyness kicks in. I allowed myself to be bossed into a position on the pitch that was not my usual position, a defensive position. I knew I was a good defender, but I knew I could shine in my real position and showcase my skills, the reason I had been chosen to attend on the day. I allowed myself to be told what to do by other people, strangers, girls I'd never met before maybe slightly older and more confident than me. I hadn't performed and I knew I did not have my best performance. But that day, I allowed social awkwardness, lack of assertiveness and anxiety to get in my way. I also learned another valuable lesson that day: Football was ruthless and life could be tough when you only got one shot at things.

Chapter Five

Forty Before Forty Part One

Fast forward a couple of years, after giving birth to my first son and dedicating my time to motherhood and my first college course, sport didn't feature too much in my life. I then endured a debilitating pelvic injury during my second pregnancy which took approximately ten years to recover from. This further exasperated the lack of physical activity in my life. I became afraid to do anything too strenuous in case I relapsed. I was 'minding myself' more than anything and avoiding certain activities 'just in case.' Recovery was slow with numerous physical therapies encountered. It was one special guy who finally put that right. A highly knowledgeable, gentle, kind and understanding man, Derek Plunkett, who performed holistic Amatsu treatments and cellular healing, explaining that the cells of our bodies hold trauma over the years. Whether that be emotional or physical trauma experienced. He was highly informative and his expertise and gentle approach of allowing me control of my recovery, rather than him dictating, did the trick. Consequently, with the recovery of the pelvic injury, I began attending a dance exercise class and slowly built up the confidence to go to the gym.

That newfound confidence in the gym coupled with the elated feeling the choir was giving me and having accomplished the singing goal to a certain point (I had not sung live in a concert with the choir), I decided, one evening after watching the reality TV show, 'Ireland's Fittest Family', that, we, as a family should sign up to the TV program. We had been watching this TV program for a couple of years as a family often saying, "I think we would be able to do that." With all in agreement, we applied for the show, and within a couple of weeks, we were at the audition stage. At that time, we were all training separately, each doing our own activities in separate gyms and in other ways. This felt like something that might be nice to do as a group, with an opportunity to strengthen our bond with one another.

I received a call from the show while abroad, informing me that they had accepted us onto the show. I was in Croatia for four days for a music festival with some friends. I had travelled to Croatia alone as the others had earlier plans to explore Venice before making the trip over to the Croatian capital city. They were also planning to travel down the coast after the festival, while I would travel home, on time, to attend a national recruitment campaign for psychologists. This was the first time in my life that I had travelled to another country alone. Any travelling I had done in the past was always with my husband and children or other family or friends. I found the experience empowering. Not only from the point of not having to be responsible for others' health, well-being, and belongings, including passports (!), but freedom of choosing what time I needed to be at the airport, what I wanted to do: listen to music, have a coffee, read, or shop while I waited. I didn't have the worry of being late and missing the plane, the wrong liquids being packed, being overly delayed at security, someone forgetting something, or moody teenagers, for that matter. Travelling had gotten easier as my children had gotten older in terms of the sheer number of items babies and young children need, the worry of them crying or feeling unsettled in a confined space, or how they would manage the flight in terms of take-off or landing. But the teen years also came with their share of difficulty. In my family, keeping male adolescents fed was important as this had a direct correlation with their mood. The timing of flights was also key. Book an early morning flight and be prepared for torture! What I realised about myself was I had been an anxious flyer in the past but not from the idea of take-off, landing or any worry about the plane dropping out of the sky. More from the fact the person that I most travelled with liked to play with time, squeezing every ounce there was out of time. Leaving zero window for any eventuality. Now, this in and of itself is not a problem, especially if partnered with someone else who equally has no problem implementing the same practice. But pair it with someone who prefers to have a little extra time, and disaster strikes from an elevated anxiety point of view.

On the bus returning to the airport in Croatia, I got chatting to a young woman from Belgium. She had also attended the music festival and camped at the campsite there. I was in awe of her. She told me that she not only travelled alone but attended the festival alone and made friends while she was there!

"Wow," I said in amazement, wondering how I would cope in that situation. It seemed quite scary. I wondered if by being a parent all my adult life, I just never had the opportunity or desire to think about it, never mind act on it. Priorities are different as a mother.

In the weeks following, the filming for the fitness show started, with the first shoot at the house and in our respective gyms to capture us in action. We had stepped up our training together and our local gym, Westpark, offered us sponsorship to train there as a family. This was a fantastic opportunity for us to train together. Then came a couple of days for filming the show and participating in the physical events. Two weeks previously, I injured my Achilles tendon while training to climb up a makeshift half-pipe (an event that was always on the show as an eliminator). I was feeling nervous about going on TV, but I knew the show was not being aired for another couple of months, so I put it to the back of my mind.

Disappointingly, we got knocked out of the competition after two events. Though I think, secretly, I felt happy as I couldn't shake a niggling feeling inside me about the possibility of an injury happening to one of us on national TV. The first event involved running on a beach, with the four of us tied together by a rope. There were nineteen other families involved in the event. With four in each family, there was a big enough crowd to go up against. It was an obstacle race with the expectation to run into a certain point in the sea from the sand dunes, run back out of the water to a set obstacle, back into the water, out to a second obstacle and then run a home stretch on the sand. The obstacles were wooden structures approximately four feet in height called over-unders. The expectation was to climb over the high parts and under the low parts while all tied together and there were about three high and low sections on each. To say I was defeated before I even started was an understatement. I knew running was not my forte and especially not with the small injury I was carrying. My endurance was not great and on the sand made that even worse. Having asthma added to that, knowing that the dust from the sand could trigger an attack. I was a sprinter and with fast twitch muscles, I knew shorter, quicker events would be my thing. Hence, I was not looking forward to it.

With nerves kicking in, it was time to set off. I managed the first part well. But on the way out of the sea the second time, heading towards the second obstacle, my eldest son, who was out in front of the four of us, taking the lead, saw another family just up ahead, lift their mother and carry her. He shouted back to his dad if he thought they would be able to carry me! Instantly, I thought, "no way, I'm too heavy." Then it made me wonder if he thought I couldn't make it, if he thought that I didn't have it in me. Suddenly, my rhythm was gone. With those thoughts kicking in and more, I started to think that I wouldn't make it to the next obstacle, never mind the end of the race. The thoughts turned to, "You're not going to make it," "you can't get a breath," "you are drowning out here," "why did you think this is a good idea?" "why did you do this?" "no one forced you, you did this to yourself," "you are letting your family down," "you are the weak link."

And with that, I started to panic. My chest started to tighten, I couldn't get a breath in. Although I was still running, I began to get lightheaded. I really wanted to stop there and then to tripod, to allow air in. I could feel the loss of control over my body. It was as if there was some disconnect between my mind and my body. Had I not been tied to the others in my family, I would have stopped and sat down to try to gather myself. But instead, I continued in full panic mode. I tried to get over the four-foot barrier. This doesn't sound too high, but being 5-foot-two inches, the barrier was up to my chest and I had to climb over it, launch myself over it, while others seemed to be able to almost step over it. Not being able to get over, my eldest son had to drag me over the top and I flopped to the ground, rolling under the next under. My co-ordination was gone, my energy was low, and I had nothing left in the tank. The panic attack had taken the life out of me, I was on automatic pilot and not doing a particularly good job. Afterwards, my son compared my state to that of a heavy wet fish. He was not far wrong! I managed to run until the finish line, feeling like a ragdoll, because I was tied to the other three of my family members. When we got to the finish line, I flopped to the ground. Lying still, trying to control my breathing, I knew something was wrong, I could feel it. My face was planted in the sand, I did not care what I was breathing in, I just couldn't move. A first responder asked if I was okay. I nodded. "I just need to catch my breath," I thought. After a couple of minutes, I got up, walked around, and felt okay, though I needed a puff of my inhaler. I could tell Dylan was extremely disappointed. Dejected, the four of us chatted and stated that I felt I was not fit enough for that type of race. One of the celebrity coaches, Donnacha O'Callaghan, a retired Irish Rugby Union player, came to chat to us.

He put his arm around me and said in a lovely manner, "It was not your event but you got through it. Chin up, tomorrow is another day." Taking stock of the positive, I was happy to have completed the event by running all the way. I could have given up but I didn't.

The second event, 'Vertigo,' involved heights, located on the top of a building in the City Centre of Dublin. Now, this Dublin city building was not the tallest and Dublin city buildings are not tall by comparison to the rest of the world. However, outside, looking up at two planks extending off the top of the building, the building looked tall enough to me!

The event itself involved going up against one other family. There were two planks about a foot wide sticking out from the top of a low-rise ten-storey building. There were four flags hanging on the end of a rope, hanging off the underneath of each plank. There was one flag halfway out on the plank and the other three were at the end of the plank. Each family member must take it in turns to go out, retrieve a flag and come back in. The first family back in made it on to the next round. Upon hearing the rules or the explanation of the event, my youngest and I had the exact same thoughts. What is the best way to approach this? How would you get out to the end of the plank, get down to reach for the rope, pull the rope up, get the flag and turn around to get back in, all at speed? What we're talking about here was motor planning. So, we broke it down step by step. We even acted it out, as much as we could, in a corner of the room we were in, we pretended to imagine being on a plank. If we could imagine a step-by-step approach, we may figure out if there were any potential oversights. Having a plan can also help to settle the body and help to remain calm. If there's a plan in place, this can form part of the coping strategy. The focus can then be on keeping the body calm, allowing enough stress, eustress, for optimum performance.

The wait was the hardest because, sometimes, the wave of emotion that would come over me felt like a wave crashing against a rock. Breathing helped, along with positive self-talk. "I can do this," "I've got this." Closer to the time we started to say to each other, "we are going to enjoy this," "Let's have fun." In the process of getting harnessed up, something clicked. I wondered what the worst thing that could happen was. If I fell off the plank, the harness would stop me from falling to my death. I decided the feelings I was experiencing reminded me of waiting in line for a rollercoaster. Now, going on rollercoasters is one of my favourite things to do and a dream of mine from young adulthood was to travel around the world to the best rollercoaster locations. I love the adrenaline rush; I love the sensation in my body and I love the buzz during and afterwards. Connecting in and associating with these feelings then allowed me to feel excited about what was coming next.

Up on the top of the building and feeling pumped up, I was raring to go. I was extremely focused. I had a plan and breathing was my anchor. While I was waiting for the klaxon to go off, I quickly imagined myself completing the task. I knew what I had to do. I had already completed it in my mind, repeatedly, as I waited. All I needed to do now was manage my breathing and I could keep control of my body. As soon as I heard the signal to begin, I darted out onto the plank as quickly as possible. I instinctively dropped to a seated position, straddling the plank. I leaned over the left side, and looking down, I blocked off the vision of the ground far below and focused on the rope. Thoughts tried to creep in about the danger and reality of the situation, but I stopped them, staying focused on the rope. I pulled the rope up and grabbed the flag free. Then came the tricky part, getting up from a seated position, and turning around to get back in. Again, instinctively, I crouched on the plank from a seated position, spun on one foot, with the other leg out to the side and sprinted back in off the plank.

Reality hit, as I watched my youngest son sprint out to the end of the plank next. I closed my eyes. I couldn't watch. Suddenly, the protective mother instinct kicked in and I had a wave of, "you've sent your family out there, you've put them in danger," came over me. But the race was so fast; it was over before I had time to address it. We had lost the race and it was on to the feeling of disappointment. We performed extremely well. Unfortunately, the ropes tangled up in the wind during the race, and when Dylan, who went last, pulled up a rope, he pulled one with no flag on it. He jumped to a lying position to retrieve the rope with the correct flag. This lost him valuable seconds and the other family won by a split second. Disappointment aside, I was feeling on top of the world. I was as high as a kite. A feeling of elation, like I could achieve anything, once I put my mind to it.

Chapter Six

Forty Before Forty Part Two

A couple of weeks after the TV show filming and having gotten over the disappointment, The Choral Society invited me to sing with them at a concert event. It was an open-air event and our choir was to sing alongside many other choirs across the country. I was nervous, excited, and determined not to allow any nerves to get the better of me. But to acknowledge that those feelings were there to help me perform. After all, it was not like I was running out of the top of a building!

I sang my heart out and the buzz was immense. I was delighted with my achievement, the first opportunity to sing in a group. Research by Bath University indicated that the people who participate in a choir, enjoy a greater feeling of togetherness and being part of a collective endeavour than others involved in different social activities. The sense that we were striving for one harmonious goal was palpable. The following month, the Choral Society sent out an email from a swing band, who would be coming to play in the local theatre, inviting their members to audition as backing singers. The lead singer of the band was looking for local talent to support his act. On my high of forty before forty, I decided to say 'yes!' Feeling I needed to be a 'yes woman,' like Jim Carrey in the film, 'Yes Man,' and just go with the flow to prolong or continue this newfound confidence or sense of empowerment bossing back was giving me, I returned my answer by email on impulse. Even though the thoughts of an individual audition terrified me, I decided to just go for it and I could always opt out later if it was not for me. I imagined myself up on a stage, like one of Diana Ross's Supremes, in a beautiful gold sequin dress, gloves above the elbow, bouffant hair and a pencil microphone. I loved that music and often thought about music and the fashion of the 1950s and 1960s and how I would have loved to have lived in that era. I thought if I were to get called to audition, it was meant to be, and I let it go. Over a week later, without giving it a second thought, an email appeared in my inbox.

The reply was an offer to audition with a choice of songs to practice and the singer of the band said he would be in touch with a date and time to attend the rehearsal. I immediately got a wave of mixed feelings of panic and excitement. I clicked the link to the songs given and began singing along to check if I was able to sing them. To my surprise, I could manage the songs. Then, all I needed to do was learn the words and melody, and practice, practice, practice. Easy… right? The worry of the uncertainty of the audition started to kick in. I wondered who was going to be there. What was it going to look like? Was there going to be a stage? Was there going to be a group of people? Were you auditioning in front of everyone? How many judges? Am I even good enough to go there? I could feel myself start to spiral and the familiar sensation of anxiety bubbled inside. I could see how quickly this could get out of control and decided to stop it dead in its tracks. I decided to give myself a pep-talk. "Nope, we are not going there, all these environmental conditions in terms of the audition are out of your control. You will not know any of that until the day. You need to just focus on practising your songs, as that is what you do have control of. Now, back to singing."

The audition crept up fast, within two days, in fact. In hindsight, I don't think there was enough time to allow anything to build. Rather, just stay in the moment and enjoy the experience. Inside the theatre, climbing up a wide staircase to the audition room, I could feel my legs go jelly-like beneath me. With each step, I said an affirmation... "I am going to enjoy this," "This feels good for me right now," "This is a pleasant experience," "What an amazing opportunity," "It doesn't matter the outcome, getting to audition is pushing the fear barrier and that's good enough." By the time I got to the top, with each ascending step, I was feeling more excited than nervous. I remembered my favourite meditation, 'Meet Your Guardian Angel,' by an Irish woman called Marian (whose surname escapes me). My mother had lent it to me some years back, suggesting I might like it or find it useful. She's resourceful like that. As a holistic practitioner and complementary therapist, most of my self-care practices had been down to her connections and ideas. I listened to this meditation often during my undergraduate psychology days. I claim it was one of the things that got me through that tough time. The meditation guided you to meet and chat to your own guardian angel, to ask their name and to ask them a question. Having met mine and finding out their name, consequently, I had been able to connect in regularly to ask for personal guidance. Like many relaxation techniques, this meditation guides you to descend a set of steps to a beautiful courtyard, and with each step counting down, you become deeper and deeper into relaxation. This time, in the auditorium, I drew on that experience. Instead of becoming more relaxed as I descended, I became more relaxed as I ascended. Stepping into that of excitement and enjoyment, with the ability to be able to cope well at the moment.

I saw a woman standing in the foyer at the top of the steps and I asked if she was there to audition. She said, 'yes,' and that another woman had just gone in and she was waiting. We got chatting and she said she was a member of a choir years ago and wanted to get back into something. She said she was nervous and I could feel her nervous energy radiating from her. In my head, I acknowledged her nervousness and decided that's where it belonged, with her. I consciously did not take it on. All too easily I could have been swept up in her emotion and found I was out at sea without a lifeline. I placed my hands on my tummy, one on top of the other. This was a technique I had learned in a Tai Chi class several years earlier. The theory is, it can stop emotions from rising from the stomach, helping to stay calm and can stop emotions radiating from oneself. I had found it worked in the past and decided to use this little tool. Every little helps!

A woman then appeared from the audition room. I knew I hadn't seen her at choral society rehearsals before. Looking extremely confident walking towards us, as if in slow motion, I found myself mesmerized by her bouncing, full head of fiery locks. She looked amazing, rock chick-like and when she opened her mouth to talk, dulcet tones leapt out. She described the audition as enjoyable and easy. The other woman with whom I was waiting, whispered, "we might as well go home now!" She was then called in next. I found myself alone with this wonderful woman and in complete awe of what she was telling me. She had been a choir member for a few years, although not presently. She was a lead singer in a female swing band and handed me her business card. Well, that blew me out of the water, with no lifeline in sight! I could feel the panic begin to wash over me. "What am I doing here?" "I am so inexperienced by comparison," "This guy is going to laugh out loud at me!" This woman was soon on her way and I found myself alone in the foyer. I had a choice. I knew to perform well I needed to be as calm and relaxed as possible. If I allowed these thoughts and feelings to take over,I would be sabotaging myself before I'd even begun. I took three deep breaths and settled myself. I told myself that it was perfectly normal to feel nervous under the circumstances. I also reminded myself that I needed a few nerves for optimum performance, and yet again, it was not as if I was running out on top of a building with or without a harness!

On my way into the audition, the lead singer of the band introduced himself as Bobby Mac. Looking around the room, it was a small auditorium with a small, floor-level stage. I saw he was the only person there and this put me at complete ease. He asked me how I was and he made a funny joke, making me laugh, putting me further at ease. He asked me broad questions and then we got to the singing part! I sang two songs out of the choice of four he had suggested to rehearse. The feedback he gave me was positive. He told me that I was a lovely singer with good range and good tone. He also suggested that I did not realise how good I was. He reported that he had a couple more people to hear and would give me an answer in a couple of days. Well, to say I was delighted was an understatement. Getting through the audition and getting that feedback was enough for me. I wasn't hung up on the outcome, more overjoyed at the achievement, yet again.

A few days after the audition, I received a response via email. Bobby selected me to be his backing singer with another woman. Mixed feelings washed over me. Excited on the one hand, I was unsure that it was really what I wanted to do. Old fears started to creep in. What if I opened my mouth to sing while on stage and nothing comes out? I also wondered who I would be singing with. It took me two days to reply because I really wanted to think hard about if this was something I thought I could do. It was less than twelve months ago that I started singing lessons and only seven months ago that I joined the choral society. I decided I had gotten that far; I might as well go for it. It could be something else I could put on my forty before forty list!

It was a brief time between finding out I was up and the show itself, perhaps only five days, with one rehearsal in between. We had a couple of days to practice the songs through and attend our first rehearsal. At the rehearsal, I met the woman I was to sing with, Aidín, the chairperson of the choir. The two songs we were due to perform were, 'Things' by Dean Martin and 'That's Life' by Frank Sinatra. I knew 'That's Life' as a song but I needed to really listen and learn it from a backing singer's perspective. I was not familiar with the other song, so I was learning that pretty much from scratch. I completely focused on learning the two songs with them on repeat constantly in my ear on my headphones at any break or transition during work and any other spare minute throughout the day. I often got pangs of, "what if I forget the words?" and gave myself a quick pep-talk each time. I knew I needed to stay focused and learn the songs. I knew my confidence would grow from learning them.

Some four years back, when I was still a manager of a preschool, I was asked to present a small component of a larger presentation for work. Presentations were not usually part of my work, but our service had been one of eleven services nationally to have participated in an initiative funded by Atlantic Philanthropies looking at positive outcomes for young children. As part of the completion of the initiative, all services involved were invited to the Mansion House in Dublin to present their findings and outcomes of their projects. Our service's project was about the professionalisation of a manual, a certified training module for staff. As I delivered the module to the staff, the researcher and project coordinator asked me to present my findings anecdotally. I was nervous. The researcher and the coordinator of the project were the main presenters. I had one or two slides as aids to prompt my speech and I spent quite some time practising it. I am someone who needs practice, practice, practice. If I have a script, I am okay. Ask me to stand up and adlib and I will freeze. Over the years, I had gotten better at being in the spotlight. With practice and rote learning, I became less nervous. I could feel the tension building right before our time to go up on stage. I quickly went to the bathroom and found I did not need to use it. Most likely because I had been plenty of times already in the past hour. "It's just nerves," I told myself. In the cubicle, I used the time to take three or four deep breaths. "This is happening," I said to myself. "There's no backing out now. Two other presenters are relying on you," "Come on, you can do this, be brave," "You've got this," "You are talking from your experience, if you forget a piece of what you are going to say or it varies slightly from the script, it's okay. No one knows what is on your script anyway." I gathered myself and found myself up on stage in seconds. When it came to my turn at the podium, I found a sense of calm wash over me. I spoke well and gave a good account. Not only was the sense of relief immense but the sense of achievement also. I received positive feedback from my team and others outside my team. To my surprise, someone asked me if I was a public speaker. Holding back a chuckle, I said 'no'. In my head, I laughed, "Me, a public speaker, the stress of that!"

From as far back as I can remember, I always found new social situations or being in the spotlight embarrassing. The earliest memory I have of being on stage, was when I was five or six-years-old. It was the school talent show. I decided to recite a poem dressed up as a clown. Our school had a large newly-built, physical education (PE) hall with a stage, full curtain, lights and backstage. Standing on stage and upon finishing the poem, I was overwhelmed by the applause. The sheer volume that came at me was immense. I looked down at the microphone and noticed there was red lipstick from my painted clown face embedded in the silver crevices of the microphone. I must have practically eaten the microphone not realising I didn't need to stand so close! I looked to my right, to my lovely teacher and whispered worriedly, "I've got lipstick on the microphone." To my surprise, the audience erupted with laughter. I remember the embarrassment and cringe feeling all too well. It was only years later reflecting on that time, I realised that the audience was laughing at my cuteness; a cute little girl saying this. In my mind, they were laughing at the act of getting lipstick on the microphone and that stayed with me for a long time.

Another memory of being in the spotlight was when I was eight-years-old. At my baby brother's baptism, my parents asked me to read a reading in the church. Having had the microphone adjusted for my height and taking a deep breath, I began reading. During the reading, I accidentally read the same line twice. I had made a mistake. I immediately froze on the spot, got extremely embarrassed and could feel myself panicking. Milliseconds felt like hours with all eyes on me. I looked over at the priest and he signalled me to continue. Awkwardly and shyly, I continued, holding back the tears. I felt like I had let everyone down and I had spoiled the reading. I said to my mother afterwards about what had happened and she replied that she didn't notice and thought that nobody else had noticed either. That relieved my feelings somewhat but I thought she was possibly just being kind.

Now standing close to the silver microphone at the sound check on this occasion, I got a flashback to the exact moment of the bright red lipstick on the mic. I remembered not to stand too close this time! I had never sung like this before or had a sound check. Watching other singers rehearse from the side stage, I saw how confident they were at the microphone. How at ease they seemed to be, to belt out a number, smile and be pleased with their performance. I could feel the shyness start to creep in. "What was I doing here?" I asked myself. Again, "Why?"

"Why do this to yourself." But again, in response to the chatter, I said, "Nope, not today Zurg," in a funny Buzz Lightyear from Toy Story voice inside my head. I took a deep breath and rose to the challenge. I had chatted to Aidín earlier that afternoon about my past nervousness at being in the spotlight. Before we went on, waiting backstage, I could feel the anxiety rising from the pit of my stomach and I began pacing. Aidín asked if I was feeling nervous and I nodded. Having her there put me at ease and we knew we could support each other if either of us got stuck. Suddenly, we were being introduced and we faltered at who was going out first. "This is it, no turning back now," I thought. Smiling, standing at the microphone, Bobby Mac interacted with the audience, chatting, and joking. The spotlights were bright and it was only possible to see the front row. Next, the music started and we began singing. Before I knew it, it was over, and we walked off the stage. We were pleased with our overall performance. It was nerve-racking yet exhilarating and fun. The two songs we sang were recorded. On the replay of the video, my arm looks like it's at a funny angle. I'm holding it slightly out away from my body. When I put myself back in that moment, and what I didn't notice at the time, was that my body seized, almost, on one side. I am holding myself rigidly. I remember noticing this, some two years or so before, in a group photo of me with my classmates on the day of our graduation ceremony. In the photo, my left arm, and in particular, my left wrist is at an awkward, unnatural angle. It seems it's what my body does when I'm extremely nervous. It completely tenses up going rigid-like. After seeing this now, and remembering then, I couldn't help but home in on it, watching specifically for it on the video.

The next month, the choral society permitted me to participate in a concert occurring in Ulster Hall in Belfast. They had performed in concert with the Belfast Philharmonic Choir a couple of months earlier, the one I had watched instead of performing in. Purportedly, I had rehearsed and worked hard enough to participate this time. One of the pieces was Carmina Burana by Carl Orff, an absolute favourite of mine and a complete privilege. I had seen this piece performed live by André Rieu and the Johann Strauss Orchestra in Maastricht less than eighteen months ago, with spectacular fireballs igniting with every gigantic cymbal crash. There were not going to be spectacular fireballs, but the same rush of excitement came over me with the thought of participating in this piece. I managed the thoughts in my head, ensuring they were positive ones and there were some slight performance nerves, which was to be expected. The experience was amazing and breathtaking and one I will treasure forever. I enjoyed every minute of it and the debrief afterwards with the group over a drink was fantastic. The elated feelings stayed with me for quite some time. Finally, it felt like I was getting somewhere, getting a grip on this anxiety piece. This was such an achievement many could take for granted.

Chapter Seven

Internal Conflict

Up to now, we have examined my life in the twelve months prior to my illness from the outside and I have shared glimpses of my thoughts and where they can bring me. As mentioned before, the version or perception of my life others may have had was entirely different to what was going on, on the inside.

By that time, I had finished a Master of Arts degree, a two-year full-time programme to become an Educational Psychologist. The dream job I was striving for, for ten years. I had given up a full-time job to return to college full-time, and with one source of income, things were tough. My family made sacrifices for me to go back to college, and boy, did I feel that guilt as a mother. I knew it was temporary and I battled through, knowing that it would come good in the end. I could see the end result, the steady well-paid state pension job as opposed to the community, non-pensioned job that I had left. A job that was battling lower demand versus higher supply in the locality. Staff had already taken a pay cut in the year previously and there was a strong concern looming of cuts to hours from full-time work to part-time work. It was not that I had any disrespect for the profession or the community work, which has always been my passion. I just had this passion and drive to move in a different direction with my life. Having a state pensionable job working with children as a psychologist had become the dream.

Several years earlier, long before the Master's degree, a psychologist, Dr Sara O'Byrne, from the local state health clinic had visited several children, over time, in the preschool for observation. As the manager and key contact, I had the pleasure of liaising with her. I was in awe of her, her presence, her knowledge, her poise, and approach. It was from there that my dream to do her job became alive. She was my inspiration, my aspiration to become a working psychologist.

The month I graduated from college, the state health organisation changed the criteria for hiring psychologists and half of my class graduated without the eligibility to be employed by this health organisation. I was one of the graduates to fall into that not-eligible category. With no job to return to, unlike other graduates in my class who had taken a career break, the fight was on to establish myself as an eligible candidate for employment. After all, this was my dream. It was a devastating blow, like sand slipping through my fingers, my dream felt like it was becoming further away than closer to me. Thinking that graduating was the achievement, with the next step preparing for interview, the next step was, in fact, seeking employment to count towards the correct amount of experience, just to be eligible for the state health sector. It took nine months to be hired by an organisation willing to take me on a temporary contract without the required days. Within that time, I often wondered if I would ever make it as a working psychologist. Over the following nine months and running myself ragged with long-distance travel to employers that would take me on, I finally had achieved what some of the other class graduates had managed to leave the course with. Though it had taken its toll—I was exhausted.

I was also struggling with the uncertainty of staying in my marriage. Feeling that we had drifted apart, each with different priorities and expectations now in comparison to when we had first met so many years ago as teenagers. I couldn't help but feel that there was something different for my life but then that only perpetuated the negative thoughts; "You are selfish," "Who do you think you are, wanting a full-on career and more?" "You are not a proper mother," "Was it not good enough to have had the opportunity to go to college and now you are still not happy?" "Why am I still not happy even now I am a working psychologist?" and on and so forth. Feeling trapped, helpless, and continuously focusing on the how: how could I get out of the big hole I fell in, where would I live, what would happen with my children, would they hate me? It all just forced me lower, further into the depths of despair.

Psychotherapist, Derry McDermott, the best one I have ever had, the most charismatic, eccentric, knowledgeable yet humble person I know, liked to use props to illustrate her point. She once said to me, while holding a butterfly pendulum and a small container in her hands, "Simone, you are not an even-keeled sort of person. You have extreme experiences. You can soar really high and then dive into a bucket of shit, soar really high, then another bucket of shit, really high and another dip in the shit." While gesturing the pendent in and out of the container at the same time. Well, this time, I was not knee-deep in it, I was practically going under, full body, head and all, and I was unsure how I was ever going to get out again and feel better. With Derry in retirement eighteen months at this stage and having tried other therapists, unsuccessfully, I was floundering. I was not the perfect wife I had strived to be for twenty years or so. The guilt I felt about the uncertain end of my marriage was overwhelming. I was not proud of this and I was allowing it to define me, to consume me.

About four weeks after the choral society concert, and just after the backing singer gig, I started having panic attacks in the month leading up to the TV show being aired. The panic was related to the programme being watched nationally. I was anxious and worried about what was going to be shown. Being quite a private person, I was feeling very exposed. A lot of old feelings began to emerge.

At the age of fifteen or sixteen, I had been badly bullied, including a physical attack by some girls. I was then unable to leave the house for fear of this happening again or bumping into anyone who may have known what had happened. Because I was attacked on my way home from school, I decided the best thing to do was to change my route to school. This meant walking part of the way, getting a different bus, and walking another part of the way. I would arrive at school two minutes late every day but that meant missing the crowd. It meant it was more predictable for me. I could go straight to my locker on an empty corridor instead of a crowded one and I did not need to look over my shoulder. Every day on my way home from school, I was on super high alert. I would not be caught out, off-guard again by anyone. I watched for every person on either side of the road. I scanned for danger constantly. I even crossed the road over and back at times if there was something up ahead that I was perceiving as dangerous. I began imagining all the potential possibilities, all the possible outcomes, and all the viable solutions. There was a lot of shame that came with that beating. I was embarrassed that I froze, stood still, and didn't fight back. I was embarrassed that I collapsed to the ground, shaking uncontrollably with shock. I was embarrassed that it happened at a bus terminal, where the bus driver got off and covered me with his coat, and later, wondered how many people sitting on the bus witnessed it. Consequently, that stayed with me for several years afterward. I did not tend to walk in my own locality alone. If I had to go somewhere, I would scan the shop or location to check it was 'safe' before I could enter. I did not want to see anyone I knew from that time, as it would evoke feelings of shame, insecurity, and embarrassment. I also worried in case there were any further altercations. It became a huge fear and a panic-inducing time. If at any time, I felt I was in danger of that, I would leave or avoid the situation.

With these old feelings rearing their ugly head again, I felt like I was right back there. I was worried about how we might be portrayed on TV and I felt extremely exposed. With the show airing and everyone seeing it, I was somewhat relieved. But it seemed this was short-lived.

The panic attacks continued. I was working hard and I began staying an hour late after work every day. I was convincing myself that the extra time I was working could go towards my holiday in the coming March. I was going to the Special Olympics World Games in Abu Dhabi and Dubai to support my brother who was representing Ireland in Basketball. But I think there was an element of not wanting to be at home, avoiding the scrutiny of any questions that might come my way about wanting to stay in the marriage or not. My head hurt any time I talked about it or anytime I had to come to a decision. I was scared for my future and staying late at work was a distraction, if not a stressful one.

On the one hand, I thought I was looking after my mental health. I was going to the gym as I said—physical exercise is good, right? But I was using the 'gym-high' as a distraction or form of relief. It became extreme in that I could attend a gym class in the morning, which set me up for the day, but then, because my work was so hectic and stressful, I would go to the gym in the evening again to feel the relief and 'gym-high' I would get. I was seeking healing often. I had weekly reflexology sessions in the month prior to my illness. I was attending weekly art therapy, and a week before the event, I had attended an Amatsu session with Derek. But there was something that I couldn't seem to shake off. I couldn't put my finger on it. As much as I was doing, I just didn't feel right. A sense of something looming but I did not know what. Two weeks before 'the event,' I was having stress headaches, but I put it down to work-related stress. On the Monday, four days before it happened, I felt pressure across my eyes, as if they were swollen. I looked like someone with hay fever, a seasonal allergy. But being winter, I put it down to the possible start of a sinus infection. I was feeling irritable and unsettled, edgy, like a nervous tension in my body. Three days before the event, in a gym class, I became breathless, light-headed and I wasn't sure if I wanted to vomit. I felt a disconnect between my mind and body and it reminded me of the race on the beach. I took my water bottle, inhaler and nodded to the instructor that I was heading towards the door, I took a breath, a drink, a puff of my inhaler, calmed myself down and headed back in for more. I put it down to not being fit enough. Two days before the event, having lunch with colleagues in our usual café, the café was unusually noisy. I was susceptible to finding the acoustics of environments difficult given the mild hearing loss in my right ear. I had a headache and found paying attention and concentrating on what my colleagues were saying difficult. I noticed I was rather quiet and thought maybe I was tired, or my hearing was bothering me more than usual. The day before the event, I worked hard in work, and as I was off on leave the following day, I challenged myself to tick all the items to do on my list. Staying late at work again, I completed all the work I had on my list, apart from printing a report, due to the printer deciding to give up on life halfway through the day. I was feeling annoyed and agitated as I couldn't tick that off my list. It also meant it had a knock-on effect to tick one or two others off the list also. I really wanted that list clear before leaving for the weekend. I had always made lists and enjoyed ticking them off, and anything I didn't do I could put on the list for the following day. But these past two months, I had almost become fixated on ticking items off the list. I would sometimes put more items down on the list, which was almost a weekly job list, and I was expecting myself to get it done in the day. There seemed a pleasure in it and quite the opposite when it was not achieved.

Chapter Eight

Initial Recovery

Back to the event that fateful night; I decided not to join the infinite serene corridor of energy. In this near-death experience, I didn't see my life flash before me or bright lights calling me. I had a choice, and at that moment, I chose to stay in my body at the top of the corridor. The answer I gave was that I felt I had more to do in my life here on earth. There was no big eureka moment about what I was supposed to do or to do differently. Just a knowing that I was meant to stay, and it was not my time to go.

The wait for the ambulance to take me to the other hospital seemed long. My husband later told me of a staff discussion he could hear just outside the curtain about what member of staff would travel in the ambulance with me. It went something like this: "if she bleeds again on the way over, it doesn't really matter who is in the ambulance with her, there is nothing you can do for her." He recounted that to be quite a shocking conversation to overhear and understandably so. The ambulance journey was horrendous. I was waning at this point and still shivering. I was freezing. I could feel every bump on the road, and with every bump, my head seemed to rattle, sending the pain cascading around my head. The sound of the siren was piercing. "Just hold on until you get there," I kept telling myself. When I got to the other hospital, it seemed warmer almost immediately and I stopped shaking. There was some commotion and I had the sense I was moved about. I was coming and going from consciousness. Feeling like I was placed in some sort of scanner, suddenly, I became hyper-aware of my arm. I thought the scanning machine had trapped my arm. I felt deep pressure and pain around my upper arm and I began screaming, thinking my arm was caught in some way. Staff rushed to my side to discover it was a blood pressure monitor going off on my arm! I must have gone unconscious again as I have no further recollection of the scanning machine or that time.

The team caring for me booked me in for a 'coiling' procedure. A coiling procedure is an endovascular procedure where a catheter is placed into the femoral artery in the groin. This is fed through the body into the brain, to the site of the ruptured aneurysm where small platinum coils shaped like a spring are deployed. An angiogram is used to detect the exact site of the rupture. This is a procedure which involves placing dye into the artery. The coiling treatment can be used to treat ruptured or unruptured aneurysms; a ruptured aneurysm, in my case.

There were many highlights during my stay in hospital mainly related to the effects of pain medication.

Upon waking from the procedure, I remember seeing my mother. I told her I had just got 'my ovaries done.' I could feel a tug in my groin and I believed getting my ovaries removed made sense for the sensation I was feeling. She laughed and said, "Did you?" and then asked if I knew what hospital I was in. I told her I was in "Crumlin."

"Crumlin, the children's hospital?" she exclaimed.

"Yeah," I said. There was something familiar about where I was. I'm not sure if it was the blue curtains against the brown windows that reminded me of that hospital or the woozy sensation of the anaesthetic that was reminding me of the last time I felt that way, when I was twelve-years-old getting a tonsillectomy. I came to realise quickly that it didn't make much sense that I would be in a children's hospital.

But still, having gotten over this little blip about where I was and what procedure I was having done, I was in top form and feeling mighty! One of the first questions I asked Paul was if he cancelled my eyelash appointment.

"I don't think you should be worrying about that right now," he replied.

"No, no. My reputation is at stake here. You can't go around making beauty appointments and not show up," I said zealously. "That sort of thing will get a girl a bad name," I thought. Paul confirmed that he had indeed cancelled the appointment and I relaxed after hearing the salon was okay about it.

Later that evening, my friend, Silvija, came to see me. She had cycled all the way over from her house to the hospital when she heard the news and I thought she was fantastic for that. She brought me a few essentials including some chocolate. I tucked into a chocolate and raspberry flavour crispy bar of chocolate. It tasted like nothing I have ever tasted before in my life. I felt like Charlie in 'Charlie and the Chocolate Factory' tasting something specially made by Willy Wonka himself. It felt like popping candy bursting with flavour with every bite, and it was setting my mouth alive with the experience.

"Mmm… this is delicious… I'm having an orgasm in my mouth," I said to Silvija, and she burst out laughing. I wasn't quite sure what she was laughing at, I was very serious. This felt like one of the most amazing experiences of my life!

Later that night, I hallucinated that the gentleman patient in the bed next to mine had been strapped to the bed without his consent. I could hear him mumbling that he needed the toilet and being told to stay in bed. He seemed somewhat disorientated and distressed and this had been happening repeatedly for some time. Being a psychologist and given my line of work, I thought that he could benefit from a support plan. I really wanted to get out of the bed to help him, but I could barely lift my head off the pillow. Upon hearing the Velcro noises and what sounded like a struggle, I imagined his wrists being velcroed to the sidebars of the bed. I convinced myself he was being restrained. Restraint is serious in my line of work, with my organisation having a strict policy with a Restraint Committee to oversee applications of the potential risk of restraint. So, in my head this was critical, and I was very concerned about this vulnerable man. I had to do what I could to help. As if this was my only mission in life, like I was Marvel's Private Investigator, Jessica Jones. Since I couldn't get out of bed myself, I called the nurse to report what I thought was happening to the man. I even asked for the hospital's restraint policy! After some debate, I could see the nurse was becoming impatient. I thought this was because I was uncovering the maltreatment of a vulnerable patient. But when the curtain between the two beds was pulled back, it revealed that the patient was wearing mittens with Velcro straps to stop him from removing a drain coming from the top of his head.

"Ohh, sorry," I said. The nurse nodded abruptly, pulled the curtain, and walked off. Oh dear, not the Jessica Jones moment I was hoping for!

The second evening, thinking I just needed a week off from work and I would be back to continue the rest of the assessments and appointments I had booked in, I sent a text message to a colleague, whom I knew to be diligent, to ensure the appointments were cancelled. I could see my diary visually in my mind and I had a full diary. I was worried that the client would show up unknowingly to a cancelled appointment and that was unacceptable in my eyes, even under the circumstances.

"I think you might need longer than a week off," Paul said. "No, no, I'm fine. I'll just take the week off and I'll be back at the gym also." Confident that was all that was needed, I imagined my diary reshuffled for the following week and I imagined walking back into the gym to keep my fitness on track. That night, as I stirred from restless slumber, I believed there were gremlins running around the ward and under the beds. For anyone who doesn't know, 'Gremlins' is a film that was out in the 1980s about Mogwai which were small, cute creatures of unknown origin. There were some rules to looking after them: do not expose them to sunlight, do not let them drink water or let them near any water, and do not feed them after midnight. If any of the three rules were broken, the Mogwai multiplied and produced nasty creatures called gremlins. As it was approximately just past midnight and I could hear a party-like atmosphere with people singing happy birthday, I was convinced that the gremlins appeared because birthday cake had been eaten and they were partying in some room at the end of the ward. I didn't actually see any gremlins, but I saw their shadows and the curtains blowing as they passed, and I was sure that was them. I lay stiffly in the bed worried and then reminded myself to relax as I could deal with them if they appeared. The following morning, speaking to the nurse, she told me that my pain medication needed to change as it was making me hallucinate. There was, in fact, a birthday for one of the nurses and they did celebrate and eat cake at midnight, but there were no gremlins!

On the third evening, my friend, Silvija, came to visit me again. She took one look at me and asked, in her Croatian accent, "What is wrong with your face, you look like a frog." My face was swollen, particularly around my eyes and forehead and there was a concern about me developing hydrocephalus, fluid on the brain. I was in terrible pain and lay listlessly as she tried feeding me some of her homemade pizza. She reported to me sometime later that she thought that I was going to die that night after seeing how poorly I was. I had a lumbar puncture the next day to try to release or reduce some cerebral spinal fluid, but it was unsuccessful. For the most part, the pain was horrific and I writhed in the bed coping minute to minute. The observation questions every thirty minutes, asking, "What's your name? What year is it? What hospital are you in?" was frustrating, especially amidst an extreme pain episode, where it was difficult to speak. I imagined recording my answers on a recording device and playing it every time would be easier than answering. But I talked to myself about this being physical pain that would pass eventually and how I had been through worse events in my life. "This is physical, you will heal," I said. "There is nothing to be scared of." That evening, my friend, Denise, who is an excellent nurse, came in to visit. I told her in a whisper that I didn't think I was in the correct ward. That I felt like I was taking up a bed that someone more in need might require.

To which Denise responded, laughing, saying, "Simone, there's a 'Falls Risk' sign above your bed, I think you are in the right place." I couldn't help but feel that there was someone more in need, at the time. Most likely a conditioned response, especially from an Irish perspective. Being raised in a Catholic school, helping others before yourself is drummed into you. But I also believed that the 'falls risk' signs were probably there permanently and not especially for me!

On reflection, I think I had overheard the nurse say that I would need about a week to recover from the coiling procedure and that was where I got that I just needed a week off work. I'm sure now that she meant I needed a week in the High Dependency Unit, as, sure enough, on the seventh day, I was able to get up for my first shower. I was then moved to the next room, still monitored by the same set of staff, but not to the same intense extent and the patients in that room were more alert and conversed more. I was also really motivated to get up and about and get back to the gym because it was a good outlet for me. Possibly, maybe because people around me told me I was not going back to the gym, I felt I had to prove them wrong. My mother reported that I was not going back to that gym if she had to stand barricading the doors herself. I remember rolling my eyes at her. I had an image of wrestling my mother at the gym door to get in and this made me laugh, and most likely, a little more determined!

I returned to the referring hospital after ten days in the specialist hospital. It was there that a nurse noticed I was still hallucinating on medication. At two a.m. one morning, when giving me medication to prevent vasospasms, I reported to her that, every time I blinked, I felt like I had butterfly eyelashes. She looked at me puzzled saying, "what do you mean?" And I said in a Luna Lovegood from Harry Potter voice,

"They are so lovely. Every time I blink, they move so slowly like delicate butterfly wings," waving my fingers in front of my eyes slowly in a flapping motion. The next day, my pain medication was changed again. During this week, I experienced some seizure-like activity which was probably one of the scariest times I had in hospital. One minute, I was propped up having a conversation with my parents by my bedside, and the next, my eyes rolled back in my head, my head fell backwards, and my body went rigid down my right side. I could not speak. I had a numbness down my right side and all I could do was feel the tears roll down my cheeks as my dad held me in his arms, whispering, "you're okay, Simone."

I honestly did not know what I was going to do with my life if this illness meant I was never able to work again or go to the gym again. Determined not to be debilitated by whatever was going on in my body, I decided to do some brain training games. I found that I could become easily overwhelmed with too much information or I got frustrated with myself when I knew I could do better or complete a task faster previously. I tired easily and I found that tricky. My brain just wasn't working at the same capacity as it did. I wasn't a very patient, patient! Now, if it were for anyone else, I would have compassion certainly, but I didn't seem to be very compassionate towards myself. I wanted to push the boundaries slightly to see my limits. Because I had no understanding of my newfound capacity or limitations, sometimes pushing too far had its repercussions and that was intense fatigue.

After seventeen days, on Christmas Eve, I was discharged from hospital and the first thing I wanted to do was stop for ice cream at Gino's Gelato, an ice cream parlour not too far from the hospital. I wanted a treat to celebrate leaving hospital but it was symbolic of celebrating something bigger; I was alive, free and I had survived. Surviving the ordeal to taste the ice cream was good enough for me. I got a Ferrero Rocher-flavoured ice cream in a waffle cone and it was delicious!

I spent the first two weeks at home in bed mostly, sleeping approximately twenty hours per day. Like a baby, I was able to get up for about an hour at a time. I got up to exchange presents on Christmas morning and went back to bed. I got up again to exchange gifts with my wider family and went back to bed. I got up for a little bit of Christmas dinner and had to go back to bed. But I was so grateful to be alive and with my family all the same. I came off my pain medication over the Christmas period as I was worried about becoming over-reliant on it. I also wondered where my baseline pain was at and how much medication my body really needed. I strongly disliked taking medication for the sake of it. Instead, I only took it if I really needed to.

The fatigue was rife. I was not able to do any housework. "Oh no!" I hear you say. But when you physically can't do something, it can be extremely frustrating. I had to be careful not to overdo it as this could induce headaches. Any increase in heart rate and the pulsation could be felt in my head, a head rush sort of feeling, which was not good. Although the rupture had been repaired, there was a fifteen percent chance the procedure would not be successful; the coils could compress, creating another leak. This would mean further surgery, more invasive. Still, there was an eighty-five percent chance success rate and I decided I was going to be one of the statistics falling in the eighty-five percent category.

Blood in the cerebral spinal fluid was the source of the pain. It needed to be broken down and absorbed back by the body which could take up to six months apparently. That being said, I was out walking five kilometres per day by six weeks, having built up slowly, starting with a walk around the block. I measured my physical progress based on my ability to walk and build on doing housework. I also chunked tasks, doing a task analysis. For example, having a shower, then lying down for a rest, drying, and dressing myself, then lying down for a rest, drying my hair, then lying down for a rest again. I measured my progress when I could do that task without a break or a decrease in the number of breaks required. My physical progress was halted as I was due to have a six-week check in Beaumont Hospital that got cancelled due to a nurse's strike at the time. I was worried to return to the gym without the go-ahead from the consultant. The new appointment ended up being another four months down the line, so I had to hold off any gym-going until the appointment, just to be cautious.

About four to six weeks after the procedure, actor Emilia Clarke, George R.R. Martin's Game of Thrones (GOT) star, who plays Daenerys Targaryen, Khaleesi, Mother of Dragons, announced that she had a similar experience five years earlier. The article reported her to have collapsed at a gym with a ruptured brain aneurysm. It was nearly a mirror of what had happened to me. It had happened to her between the filming of season one and season two of GOT. They had discovered she had a second unruptured aneurysm which needed to be clipped. She then had this procedure between the filming of season two and season three. She had waited to inform people of the events of her personal life as she felt she would be judged, her acting scrutinised in comparison to an earlier season. I was astounded to hear this news. I love Game of Thrones and I love the character Khaleesi! I also admired the actor Emilia Clarke and her work in the very moving and captivating film, 'Me Before You.' I found this latest announcement of her personal story so inspirational and so motivating. The launch of her charity, SameYou, only further supported my outlook. I connected with the character Khaleesi, seeing that 'the event' had happened to Khaleesi, Mother of Dragons. I thought, if she can do it, I can do it. I had thoughts about how well she looked; we never would have guessed that that was going on in her background. Looking at me six weeks on, "it can only get better," I thought. I had planned to meet colleagues for lunch that week. Mainly because I enjoyed their company, they were my friends, but it gave me motivation and a sense of purpose. We discussed her experience; how brave she was and how she had waited to announce the experience.

One colleague said, "Look what you and Daenerys Targaryen have in common!" It was said in an admiring way and I was delighted.

"Yes," I said, so proudly.

Chapter Nine

Further Recovery

Post-procedure, the journey to recovery physically was quick in that it was one which seemed to peak first and plateau by comparison to other areas. Apart from the five kilometre walks, the planned trip to the Special Olympics World Games in Abu Dhabi and Dubai some twelve weeks post-procedure was a catalyst to the physical recovery journey. I was eager to get back to health as quickly as I could, as I desperately wanted to support my brother, Geoff. The trip, booked some time ago, was a constant talking point of excitement. Not only was there an opportunity to support my brother at World Games, but there was also an opportunity to explore a new country, which was home to Ferrari World, the largest indoor theme park, with a rollercoaster I wanted to experience. In the lead-up to the trip, I wondered if I could go on rollercoasters now. I also knew that I couldn't leave the country while on sick leave from work. I had to be well enough to return to work with enough time to book the time off and leave the country. I managed to return to work after nine weeks, with some difficulty, and got to Abu

Dhabi and Dubai. I was incredibly pleased with how far I had come in such a short space of time, despite the need for a wheelchair at the airports, frequent naps, and sensory breaks during the stay. It was a proud moment to cheer for my baby brother as he represented his country in his green sports gear and one I will cherish always. We drove past Ferrari World while travelling from Abu Dhabi to Dubai, and disappointingly, watching it from afar, fading out of view, I was too unwell to go. My brain was not in a good place to take the impact of any g-force and I resigned to that. "We'll just have to come back another time," I said positively.

Back from Abu Dhabi and Dubai, on reflection, I returned to work prematurely. I was on a temporary contract which was up at the end of March shortly after I returned from abroad and I needed to show I was still capable of being a good employee to be kept on. Being fit for work, for me, meant I was well and had a purpose. From an Irish perspective, we had something called 'Invalidity Pension.' This is a payment that may be paid when an individual cannot work due to a long-term illness or disability, covered by social insurance (PRSI). Subconsciously, I had a belief, possibly from a societal perspective, that going on this pension meant I was 'invalid' as a person, compounding the need to show the world that I was now still 'valid'.

I returned to work, on my GP's advice, three days per week, Monday, Wednesday and Friday, with Tuesday and Thursdays to recover. The Occupational Health doctor, a very experienced woman in Subarachnoid Haemorrhage, having worked in the UK referring patients of this nature to the appropriate hospitals, recommended that I should do three half days as I needed, to phase back to work appropriately. My employer was prepared to support a phase back to work but not from a financial point of view. They suggested that I would only be paid for the three half days that I was there and that I could use annual leave for the rest. When I responded that I thought it was unfair, highlighting that there was a mutual benefit to me and them if I returned, they did not seem interested. They suggested I had a choice; I could be paid fully using my annual leave or build up the time as 'time off in lieu' to owe them back when I was fully fit. I couldn't understand this, and again, this seemed unfair and not conducive to a healthy recovery. After all, I had a critical illness with no idea how long this process would take or when I would be well enough to come back. Coming back full-time alone seemed so overwhelming, never mind owing them time also.

It was at this time that I opted to seek some expert support. Though I had the support of family, friends, and colleagues, I felt increasingly aware of the lack of understanding surrounding my illness. My line manager, who had visited me in hospital and linked in with me every week before I returned to work, was incredibly supportive. He was also struggling with the employer's stance on the situation and encouraged the referral for expert advice. During my educational psychology training, I remembered having lectures from psychologists working with Acquired Brain Injury Ireland, so I knew there was support out there. I did some research and self-referred to Headway, a charity organisation supporting brain injury, which was based not too far from my job.

I then appealed the decision to my employer by requesting that they reconsider on the grounds of critical illness. I waited ten weeks for a decision, spending a lot of my time when I was not in work following this up. I was hugely overwhelmed emotionally and it was becoming quite disabling. Human resources (HR) informed me that the CEO had decided to not allow me to work the phased back to work from a financial point of view. I was given a choice to be only paid for the work I was doing, use annual leave or build up time to owe them back. When I argued that, I was told that I had the choice to go back out sick. I was distraught. I felt I had wasted too much time trying to follow up on everything, getting a contract extension for a further three months, getting a review occupational health appointment, getting a decision about if I would be paid or not, all while trying to return to work to remember how to do my job. The energy would have been better spent recovering without the added burden of all that.

My employer told me that if I went to the next occupational health appointment and they approved that I had a critical illness and signed me off out sick again, then I would be backdated on full pay. In April, at the next occupational health appointment, the doctor signed me back out sick for a further eight weeks. She informed me that she couldn't approve the critical illness there and then. That was a separate appointment that my employer should have requested, as it required me to collate all my medical reports for her to review. In fairness to her, she reported that this was not okay for them to treat me like this. Which was validating as I cried hot tears of frustration. Eventually, critical illness was approved in May 2019, some five months after the event, and I received full pay without having to owe my employer any time back. Although this was a huge relief and I felt fortunate to be on full pay, I couldn't help but feel angry at how they had treated me.

Everything felt so confusing and overwhelming. I had been so worried about my job, finances, and my ability to do my job. Everything felt like it had changed. I had even noted changes to my sensory preferences since before the event. I used to be someone who woke in the morning and alerted well with opening the curtains, blinds, and windows. These days, I didn't like the light much. It stung my eyes. I needed more peace and quiet also. Noisy environments hurt my ears and my head. Even taste and certain textures in my mouth seemed different. Out at lunch one day, I remember a friend asking if I liked spinach. I just remember feeling like I had no recall of what spinach ever tasted like or what it felt like in my mouth. So, I had to find out and establish that I did, in fact, like it!

On a night out with work colleagues, we went to a Japanese restaurant. As our meals began arriving, I noticed there were only chopsticks on the table. I remember looking at the chopsticks knowing that they were utensils and that they were used to eat with, but I just stared blankly at them. I wouldn't have said that I was proficient in any way with using chopsticks, but my brain and that motor planning side just couldn't figure out what I was supposed to do with them. I could feel a bit of panic setting in. When I looked around the table, everybody seemed comfortable picking them up and using them to eat their food. I picked mine up and they just felt very alien. I couldn't figure out how I was supposed to get these things to work in my hand.

As they lay separately in the palm of my right hand, I said to one of the guys beside me, "I don't think I can use chopsticks."

With a shrug he replied, "Just get a fork!" and then he asked the server for a fork for me and that was it. No big deal. But it was a big deal for me. Because I couldn't figure out how I couldn't get my hands or fingers to remember what to do. It did feel a little scary, but more confusing than anything else. I was also having word-finding difficulties, though not noticeable to many because I wanted it that way. It was more obvious when I was tired. I would give long pauses during a sentence while I searched for the word. Often, I did a physical action or described the words I was looking for. For example, "the thing that holds the clothes on the line," while doing a pinching action with my fingers. My family members would then give me the missing word, "peg", and I would say, "peg, yes, thank you", and we would move on. But when I was extremely tired, the description could be something like, "you know, the thing for the thing", and then I would become frustrated, deflated, and just give up. In this state, my movements slowed, my words slurred and I could experience a brief feeling of shut-down.

My younger son, Owen, sometimes just said, "Are you drunk again?" and we would laugh and that would diffuse it.

Chapter Ten

Along Came Dean Donnelly

Commensurate with getting my life back on track, upon returning from Dubai, I started a life coaching course with a woman called Caroline Caffrey. The course was based on the teachings of Bob Proctor, predominantly, but with reference to other great teachers also. It was at this time that I started to look at what I genuinely wanted for my life and how I wanted to live that life, especially post-near-death experience. In studying this material, I realised that I had lost skills, small tips, and tricks I had picked up along the way that I had forgotten about. This course really helped me to recall tools I had used in the past, but it also enlightened me about many new things I had yet to discover about myself. During an exercise on productive and non-productive actions, the expectation was to review some part of your life, exploring some effective and not-so-effective ways we might go about things. I started with something reasonably simple. Yet, it was in this simple activity that I identified how negatively I was talking to myself in such a self-sabotaging and destructive way. I chose to look at my chocolate addiction. For the most part,

I felt in control, but when the sugar craving hit, I was like a gremlin after midnight, scavenging, raiding the cupboards on the hunt for something sweet. I noticed that, every time I 'sneaked' chocolate, I was saying horrible declarations to myself about what I had done, commenting on my ways and my inability to have self-control over sweet treats. Immediately, I put a stop to that language towards myself but I wondered how much more I was saying to myself in other scenarios of which I was completely unaware.

That was only one small exercise of many, and as I started to focus on imagining being back to full physical health, what that looked like and writing my gratitude about it, I began having urges to get the support of a personal trainer to help get me back to fitness. Although I desperately wanted to get back to fitness, I knew that I needed some help with it. I was worried to go back to the gym where I collapsed. I felt maybe I would be monitored by staff and I also wondered if I would be able to go back there, psychologically. These urges developed into the idea of wanting to speak to Paddy Holohan, the retired Irish UFC fighter. My son, Owen, attended Paddy's Mixed Martial Arts (MMA) gym and Paddy was one of his coaches. Feeling nervous about it, one evening upon collecting Owen from a session, I decided to just go for it.

I asked Paddy if he had a minute, and being his generous self, signalled me to sit on the bench beside him. I explained my experience to Paddy and he listened intently.

He said, "That was you?" sounding surprised. "You were the one who had a stroke in that gym? Simone, that was big news!" "Was it big news?" I thought. But it was more the word 'stroke' that irked me. He proceeded to tell me a little about his own stroke story and we both laughed at our experiences of near-death magic! Paddy said that he had someone in mind and that I should meet him. It was his good friend and personal trainer, Dean Donnelly. Paddy encouraged me to set up a meeting with him and I suggested it might be best I wait for the Consultant Neurologist's visit to get the go-ahead.

Paddy being paddy laughed and said, "Fuck the doctors. I wouldn't be where I am today if I listened to them!" Laughing at his contagious good-spirited nature, I felt the need to be cautious all the same.

I remember the first appointment with the Consultant Neurologist and I'm sure the Consultant remembered me! I had a list of activities that I wondered whether they were safe to do with this injury, and in an extremely excited manner, I asked, Could I jump out of a plane? Could I go on a rollercoaster? Could I do gymnastics? Could I do jiujitsu? Could I lift heavy weights? Could I go back to the gym? He chuckled and slowly gave a considered answer to each one.

Once I got the go-ahead from the consultant, I met with Paddy again. He encouraged me to come and watch a jiujitsu class.

"I'm not going to be able to do that!" I said.

"You'll love it," he said enthusiastically. Being an MMA gym, downstairs was a large mat area for striking training with an octagon cage in the corner and punching bags hanging from the ceiling. Close by the mats was a strength and conditioning area. Upstairs was a large softer mat space for jiujitsu and wrestling training, with smaller rooms off it. One room had an infrared sauna and the other was for physical therapies. Beginning here could feel daunting for some, but I had been in and out of the gym many times collecting my son and it was always a welcoming place. There was something that just felt right about being there, a kind of knowing.

It was upstairs, sitting on the sofa, that I met Dean, my new personal trainer. Little did I know at that time that, in the years to come he would be more than just a personal trainer, but a friend for life. Watching Paddy in action, I knew I wouldn't have had the co-ordination, concentration, or good reaction time, never mind the endurance and stamina required for the class.

I whispered to Dean, "I won't be able for that," sounding a little worried.

Dean smiled, nodded, and said, "I know, it's okay, you don't have to!" At our first session, Dean assessed my movement. I was terrified that he was going to tell me that I was worse than I thought I was. But he was encouraging. He asked me to do a squat and I stood and looked at him, panicked at not being able to pull the image of how to squat to mind. Dean demonstrated a squat and I followed suit. He then asked me to do a lunge, and again, the same thing happened. How embarrassing, I thought, "Why can I not do this?" But again, I watched as he demonstrated and I followed. At one point, he asked me to sidestep across the gym floor on the downstairs mat area. As I stepped out with my right foot each time, I couldn't help but feel like my leg was like a dinosaur leg. It was slow and jerky and I felt older than my years. My right arm matched the level of awkwardness. Stuck out and bent, I likened myself to that of a T-rex. I heard Dean shout across to, "Stay in the box." But I was so busy concentrating on getting my body to just move in a sidestep, super focused on the awkwardness of my movements, that I hadn't noticed I had made my way across the mats in a diagonal fashion. It was only when I got to the other side and turned to see Dean, that I realised I was at a completely different part of the wall than where I was supposed to be. I had no awareness of where my body was in space.

"How did I get here?" I said curiously. Dean commented that he had been telling me to stay inside the box. But that instruction did not land. In my head, I was staying inside the box, just not the right box adjacent to one another!

My attendance of two sessions per week began to steadily rack up. Dean focused much of the sessions on regaining movements and exploring what my body could do. I had difficulty following verbal instructions, poor motor planning and could be unbalanced and uncoordinated at times. Dean had to break a task or exercise into small steps so I could get a better understanding of the sequence of the movement. Once I had the sequence mastered, I could then speed it up and master the movement. One day, as I was chatting to Dean in between exercises, he asked me if I noticed what I was doing.

I replied, "What do you mean?"

He said, "How you are standing?" I checked myself and saw that I was unknowingly doing the yoga 'tree pose.' Dean reported that he was keeping me talking so that he could see how long I stayed in the pose. This began happening more regularly with different poses, but my favourite was pulling my leg into 'dancer pose.' This happened at home also, as if I were exploring what ways my body could move again. While sitting on the sofa, I found myself in 'happy baby pose' often, that or trying to pull my leg over my head. One session per week with Dean focused on strength training and the other session focused on mobility. I loved the mobility sessions as Dean incorporated my love of gymnastics there. It was during a strength training session, in relearning to back squat, I was feeling incredibly nervous as I approached the bar. Before my hands even touched the bar, I was feeling shaky. The worst part was stepping back from the rack. It was scary. Having no sense of where my body was in space and no control over it, this might sound dramatic, but it felt like I was like stepping off a cliff backwards. I was rattled and I needed to tell Dean. I didn't want it to take over, so much so, that I would start avoiding the session. At the next mobility session, I told him, and he said we needed to do something different, to approach it in a different way.

At times, I thought I was doing incredibly well and then something would happen where I became aware of a movement I couldn't do. One example was with mountain climbers. Dean had given me instructions and I was ready to go but then paused braced in a plank position, I couldn't figure out how to get my feet to move. It was as if they were glued to the floor. I knew I needed to move them but they just wouldn't move. I could feel my cheeks burn with embarrassment. There were a few others close by and I was cringing. Could they see how I couldn't get my body to move? Were they wondering what I was doing? But Dean got down beside me and showed me move by move, then guided me through it verbally. Before I knew it, my feet were going, I was doing mountain climbers and I was beaming.

Over time, as my ability increased and the intensity of the sessions increased, I noticed my right arm tended to fatigue more quickly than other parts of my body. I would get a numb or tingly sensation in my arm and it felt like I had no control over it. After the session, it could flop limply on my lap as I drove one-handedly back home. Some days it could take an hour to recover before it could work properly again. I was also having small, panicked feelings every time my heart rate increased. It was as if my body was remembering, making an association with what had happened before—elevated heart rate equals collapse to the floor. Every time my heart rate increased, I wanted to stop the exercise, and panicked thinking I might collapse. Dean supported me through this really well. Only he knows his methods. Sometimes he acknowledged it, sometimes he ignored it, sometimes he distracted me and sometimes he addressed it. But it worked and I got over it!

Dean not only supported me with the physical side of movement but he also helped me to look at other aspects; sleep, food intake, water intake, supplements, and hormones. Before I knew it, during the summer months, my weight was coming down and I was feeling good. So much so, that I felt able to reach out to Westpark Gym to see if I could find out about Stephen. I didn't even know his surname. I was having strong feelings to connect with him, to thank him for saving my life. In contacting Lizzie, the Assistant Manager, at the gym, to ask for Stephen's number, she asked me in for a coffee and a chat. The gym has a coffee shop on the premises and we met there. Lizzie chatted away with me, asking how I was and if I needed anything. She brought me up to the studio and we stood at the spot where it had happened. She asked how I was doing. It was strange being back there, thinking that this is where I could have taken my last breath. She was extremely supportive and I appreciated that.

Lizzie got back to me with Stephen's number and I was feeling nervous. What should I write in the text message? I thought. I texted Stephen reporting to be the person whose life he saved and asked if he could meet me. We arranged to meet in the coffee shop onsite. I had no idea what Stephen looked like and this was unnerving. I wasn't really sure what I was going to say to him, though I knew I wanted to express my gratitude and appreciation at how he had saved my life. When we did finally meet, Stephen informed me that he didn't drink tea or coffee and didn't want lunch. I felt a little bewildered as that was the least I thought I could do in exchange for him saving my life. But the conversation flowed with Stephen telling me some parts that I did not remember at all about that night, and me telling him things I could hear when I was 'gone again.' He was amazed that I knew he was going out with his friends that evening. I told him I thought they were going for a Christmas party. He told me that they were in fact going to Belfast for a Coldplay concert that weekend. They did not end up going up on the Friday night as a result of what had happened. Stephen also told me he had just completed his advanced paramedic training. How lucky was I that a paramedic was there? He had seen the commotion, come to my aid and was present with me until the ambulance arrived ninety minutes later. I told him that it was his soft voice and gentle presence that kept me calm and got me through it. Stephen escorted me up to the studio and we chatted again up there in the exact spot where it happened. It was slightly nerve-racking, but having been there with Lizzie already, I felt at complete ease with Stephen there to support me. As I stood and looked at Stephen Carass, this warm energized man who had saved my life, I couldn't help but feel incredibly grateful to him.

At the first magnetic resonance imaging (MRI) appointment, apprehension started to build, as I was not sure what to expect. I knew the only way to get through it was to keep calm. I'd been through so much already; this was surely a piece of cake. The MRI scan experience is a hostile one. The environment was loud, piercing, and painful, despite the earplugs. The mandatory wearing of earplugs is required as the noise can range from anywhere between sixty-five and one-hundred-and-thirty decibels. To put it into context, ninety-four decibels is equivalent to a food processor or blender noise. While one-hundred-and-twenty decibels is likened to a jet plane taking off, with one-hundred-and-thirty decibels like a constant jackhammer in operation. Lying back on the transport table, with my earplugs in, the radiologist secured the head cage around my head and neck. In being transported backwards through the tunnel, I told myself to stay calm and relaxed, that there was nothing to worry about. As the scanner went through the sequence and with every variation in sound and decibel, I could feel my brain twitch in various places. It did feel like a jackhammer to my brain. Though wondering what the images of my brain being captured looked like and how my brain might light up on a functional MRI (fMRI) during a task could differ from that of this scan kept me entertained. The result of the MRI, read to me at another appointment with the consultant, was positive. He reported that the treatment was successful. The scar tissue had formed at the occlusion site and the platinum coils were looking well. As I walked out of the appointment, I was well on my way to falling into the eighty-five percent success rate bracket and I was beaming.

Feeling on a roll, in September 2019, eager to return to choir practice, I joined the rehearsal. I was delighted with myself. But very quickly, I noticed that the acoustics were overbearing. My ears hurt and my head hurt. Concentrating was difficult and I could not follow along with the score as before. "Perhaps I had returned too early," I thought. Trying to manage being back at work on a four-day week and working on my physical health was enough to be getting on with. Maybe I needed to wait until I was better established with those aspects before returning. After all, singing was supposed to be fun, something uplifting not another drain on the body. Instead, I thought going back to Westpark Gym for yoga might be more doable and enjoyable. Since I had already visited there with Lizzie and Stephen, I was feeling okay to just going back for gentle exercise.

Chapter Eleven

The Mighty Fall

In October 2019, some ten months after the event, I had an interesting evening that would change how I looked at myself forever. You could say I hit my emotional rock bottom. It was a Friday night work night out to celebrate my dear friend, Ellen, leaving her post and moving on to pastures new. Some five days previous, my husband and I had announced our separation to our children. To say it was one of the most awful evenings of my life would be an understatement and my mood didn't seem to improve much as the night out drew closer. Not feeling the best, I decided to try to shrug it off and go on the night out under the circumstances. Given the emotional nature of the week, in hindsight, I would advise not to add alcohol to the mix. I had decided to start off slowly and pace myself. But lo and behold, as soon as the alcohol hit, I was on for more cocktails.

It was an emotive evening and at about four in the morning, dancing to music and swinging each other around, I accidently fell full force onto the tiled floor with my hands behind my back. In swinging forward and back,

I was moving with plenty of momentum but with not enough time for my eyes to catch up or my hands to go out to save myself, launching forward into a faceplant, nose first. I knocked myself unconscious, and as I roused from the unconscious state, lying flat on my stomach, and feeling a similar sensation to that of ten months ago on the gym floor, I went into full-blown panic mode. With the lifting of my head and the sight of the blood-stained tiled floor in front of me, I instantly made a connection that I was having another brain haemorrhage. Screaming, I asked my friends, Cara and Ellen, if I was having another brain haemorrhage. With all their endeavour they explained what had happened. An ambulance was called, and with my medical history, I was advised to stay flat on the floor, face down and not move from there. Looking out over the immediate area, the whole floor surface was carpeted a glossy red. It was through talking that I then realised I had no front teeth, which initiated a nuclear reactor meltdown.

Screaming repeatedly to Cara, "I have no fucking teeth, my teeth are gone."

She laughed, saying, "You do have teeth; I can see them!" My two front teeth had completely shattered at the back and one incisor, on the right side, was gone. Since she was on my left side, she couldn't get a clear view of the actual damage. I was very panicked, shocked, and very worried. Realising the extent of the damage, she reassuringly said that it was all fixable and I'd have new teeth in no time.

Full of emotion I said, "This is going to take me six months to recover from." My thoughts went straight to not being able to train or work out and this was a devasting blow. In the back of the ambulance, the paramedic tried giving me some pain relief to which I said no. When he asked me on a scale of one to ten where the pain was, I said it was a three.

He said "Really, are you sure? Maybe when the alcohol wears off, you might need something!" I explained that I had a brain haemorrhage ten months previous which was the worst pain of my life, including giving birth twice, marking it at an eleven out of ten, so being at a three was nothing. When he learned I had lost some teeth, he ran back into the house to gather them. But they were not salvageable at that point. No glue was going to put them back together!

Ellen came with me to the hospital and stayed with me until they discharged me. As a precaution, I received a CT scan and the Neurologist reported that all was well with my brain. I had a large hematoma on my forehead between my eyes, two black eyes, a fractured nose, three broken front teeth and a lacerated lip. It couldn't get any worse than this. When I looked in the mirror, all I saw was an Orc from 'Lord of the Rings' staring back. I was referred for an emergency dental hospital appointment that afternoon and Paul brought me. He described feeling like people were staring, wondering what had happened and if he might be to blame. He said he had urges to say aloud, "it wasn't me; she had a fall." I laughed at his discomfort, but

I was in too much shock and pain to care too much about people staring. Four hours of treatment in the dental chair later and I was free to go. They had patched me up, splinting what was left of my teeth together to try to preserve the roots and I was placed on a soft diet for a month to allow my mouth to heal.

After the weekend, I texted Dean, worriedly, to say that I had an accident and that I wasn't sure about being able to train. He wondered if I was in a cast! We arranged to meet for a coffee and I had to warn him he might be in for a shock. As I took down my hood and took off my sunglasses, I could see the shock on Dean's face.

"What the hell happened to you?" half laughing, half serious.

When I opened my mouth to speak, Dean said, "you look like a hillbilly," and we both laughed. He said he had seen fighters do rounds and come off less scathed. We had that in common at least, the ability to laugh in the face of adversity. Upon hearing what had happened, he asked me to tell him what had really happened. I told him the fall accident was what had happened and that I had witnesses! It was a good meeting. Dean advised that I could still train, I just needed to take it easy. The next day at the gym, another trainer, upon seeing me, asked if they needed to sort anyone out. I reassured him it was a silly drunken fall. He stated I was lucky I was training in a fighting gym because I fit right in there. We all laughed and I felt at ease with a keen sense of belonging. With it being two weeks to my fortieth birthday, I decided I could just add the mighty fall to my forty before forty list!

Delighted that my smashed face was not going to impede my physical recovery too much, it seemed this fall was the catalyst for finally starting to look at the emotional aspect. As a fortieth birthday present to myself, I had already booked a solo stay in Monart, an adult-only five-star spa hotel, for a nice peaceful mid-week retreat that week. During this stay, most of the time I forgot what I looked like, but I got a stark reminder when walking past a couple, smiling, and nodding in greeting, the man very animatedly jumped back two feet away from me upon the sight of me. I found this very funny and giggled to myself. But alone, with strangers mirroring their shock at my appearance, I wondered what was going on with me altogether. Had the brain haemorrhage not floored me enough? Now this. Every time I looked in the mirror, I just saw an Orc staring back.

I had also just begun attending Headway for some counselling. It was through this that I learned about the effects of alcohol on my brain-injured brain. The therapist reported that my brain most likely was having difficulty processing the alcohol by comparison to what I was able to before and I needed to be extra careful, almost learning my limits all over again. She suggested considering that having one drink, to someone without a brain injury, the effect was like having one drink, but for someone with a brain injury, one drink was like the equivalent of having three drinks. This realisation felt bleak. But I didn't have too much time to dwell on all that, I had work to get back to, some birthday party gathering arrangements to sort out and an itinerary to book for some new teeth. Silvija highly recommended Dentum, a clinic in Zagreb in Croatia to get my teeth fixed. But I had to wait a month for the trauma to subside before I could get an appointment. I became very self-conscious with my broken teeth, and although I resorted to laughter most often, I was covering my mouth with my hand, not smiling, or sucking my top lip down to hide my gappy top teeth.

I received exemplary treatment in Zagreb the following month, and with fantastic temporary teeth in place, I was feeling really good. I was delighted with the temporary result, hoping that the permanent new teeth would be just as fantastic. Though this was uncertain. Only time would tell as I needed to wait four months to allow my mouth to heal. The clinic was uncertain how the bone would heal. I was at risk of losing what was left of one of the front teeth which could have implications for certain types of treatment. Back in Dublin, a follow-up appointment with the Ear, Nose and Throat surgeon proved fruitful, and luckily, no surgery on my fractured nose was required. They reported that the bridge of my nose was now wider than it once was but that the swelling should completely reduce over the coming six months or so. With my black eyes gone, my nose on the mend, my temporary teeth in and bottom lip left with a small scar, I was feeling incredibly lucky, to say the least. Coming into the new year, reflecting on the past year, I was happy to be leaving 2019 behind and heading into 2020 in better health. Onwards and upwards!

Chapter Twelve

Languishing

Back at work, at the start of a new year, I was back to a five-day working week. The past six months, I had phased back to work on a three-day week at first, building up to a four-day week using annual leave. As I had no annual leave as such, I had no choice now but to do five days. My line manager had left some months earlier and I was being well-supported by an interim manager. Upon chatting one day, she reported that she had nursed her sister back to health after a subarachnoid haemorrhage and knew my plight somewhat. This was reassuring and it was good to chat with someone who understood.

During a neuropsychological assessment with Headway that month, the Neuropsychologist, Elaine, recommended that I consider self-compassion. I had been quite harsh on myself for not being as responsive or not responding in the same way I may have done pre-injury. I thought a little about self-compassion. But I saw self-criticism as a way to self-improve and continue on my mission proving to the world that I was 'valid' or the same 'me' as before. Though I'm not quite sure now if it was the world or myself that needed convincing. Elaine also recommended that I make a review appointment with the Endocrinology Department. When she queried my emotional health, I told her that I had been experiencing some difficult thoughts and feelings which I had tracked in line with my menstrual cycle. Approximately ten days before my period was due, I was experiencing overwhelming mood shifts, thoughts that the world was a very unsafe place, feeling isolated and lonely, yet with the need to disconnect and shut myself off from the world. I had described it to a friend one day at work like I wanted to climb under my desk and hide and not come back out. The Neuropsychologist reported that hormones and brain chemistry can be affected by brain injury and it was worth further investigation. I then requested an appointment with the Endocrinology Department, a clinic I had already been linked with in the past and awaited for an appointment.

During January and early February, the five-day week was tough. With the fast-paced pressure of my job, I needed evenings and weekends to catch up on fatigue and it all became too much. I was tired and low in self-confidence about my abilities, and as a result, I strongly considered the interim manager's suggestion of a reduction to a four-day week and applied for this support.

Slí Bleatha Float House had opened its doors in Paddy Holohan's gym just before Christmas. Seeing the float room develop, opposite the female changing room and hearing about it from Dean, I was eager to try out this new experience. The float experience combines the sensation of weightlessness with an experience known technically as Restricted Environment Stimulation Therapy (REST). Over a thousand pounds of Epsom Salts (Magnesium Sulphate) are dissolved into a human skin-temperature pool or tank of water. This super-saturated Epsom Salt solution creates a hyper-buoyant environment where users naturally float on the surface without any effort. This frees the user from the effects of gravity, facilitating a deep relaxation of the body and a state of meditative calm within the mind. "Maybe this was exactly what I needed given the deterioration in my health over the past number of weeks," I thought. Slightly worried about my heart rate becoming elevated and the type of experience I might have, I chatted to one of the owners, Pat Finlay. He suggested I would be okay and shared some of his own health and floating experience with me. Keen to try it out, I booked a session. To get the best experience, it is recommended to float naked. In getting over the initial cringe of that and preparing to get into the tank, I was fascinated to see what this experience would be like. "Here goes," I thought as I stepped in and closed the lid of the tank down behind me. Lying flat on my back, arms stretched overhead, the first feeling I had was that I was suspended in jelly. "This is so weird," I thought. In listening to the five-minute intro music with the soothing lights on, I could feel my body relaxing, almost pulsating in time to the rhythm. The music stopped, and with the lights fading out, now in complete darkness, I began floating down a river, swaying gently as I went. As I am short, my hands or feet didn't touch the walls of the tank. How easy it was to stretch my neck in this jelly-like substance, how easy it was for all my muscles to relax. It was so warm and cosy. I lost track of all sense of time and space, alone with my mind, with the opportunity to observe my thoughts as they came and went. I'm sure I must have fallen asleep as an hour passed by quickly. Getting out of the tank, I floated to the nearby shower. With the warm flow of water over my head and down my back, I didn't quite feel in my body. "Wow, floating was amazing," I thought. A post-float positive glow seemed to last for hours and was just what I needed.

Shortly after that, I travelled back to the dental clinic in Zagreb. To my delight, the bone had healed well and we could proceed with the treatment as planned. Five days later, I was back home in Dublin with my new permanent teeth, just in time, only days before COVID-19 school closures and lockdown restrictions came into place. I awaited the decision from management to grant me the reduction in hours to a four-day week, along came working from home. For the first six months of lockdown, dreaming about the float tank and how good it felt, kept me in good spirits, while going on the 'Keto' diet kept my weight under control. Between memes of alcohol and chocolate becoming our friends during lockdown, I knew I did not want to go there. As the gyms were closed, I decided to focus on my diet and started jogging in the park next door to my house. It was while out jogging one bright evening, listening to my classical music playlist for jogging, that I felt an overpowering sense of connection. Listening to 'Arrival of the Birds' (featured in the movie 'The Theory of Everything') by the Cinematic Orchestra and London Metropolitan Orchestra, as the piece rose to a crescendo and with a little momentum having sprinted over a small bridge, I looked up into the sky to see birds flying in a V-shape. As I was jogging along the path, looking up, the birds were in alignment with me overhead. Feeling a strong connection to nature and one with these birds, I had an enormous wave of positive emotion wash over me. The message was about connection and how life could only get better. When I got back from my jog, I felt the need to connect back in with Derry, though I was unsure of her response, something told me to reconnect. I sent her an email and she responded. Upon hearing my troubles, Derry opted to come out of retirement to support me and the intense therapy journey commenced.

Simultaneously, as recommended by the Vocational Support Officer with Headway, I had an Occupational Therapist (OT) assessment with the National Rehabilitation Hospital, to explore the type of support or equipment I may need at work. In describing some of my physical difficulties, balance and co-ordination difficulties, motor planning difficulties, right-sided weakness and what I noticed my hand doing as I was cutting a birthday cake, she named my difficulties as 'Apraxia,' an inability to perform familiar movements. It was a couple of weeks prior to the appointment that I noticed I was holding a knife at an awkward angle while cutting a cake. To cut the cake, my whole arm moved to cut it, not just my hand and wrist. The OT reported that can happen, giving an example of a person who stirred the sugar in their cup of tea by moving their whole body and not just their hand. I was enthralled by this. I had been saying for quite some time that my difficulties were dyspraxia-type difficulties. The OT explained that dyspraxia was a developmental difficulty from birth, but apraxia was a similar difficulty, acquired in my case. "Yes!" I was delighted with this news. This made so much sense to me. I had been talking about these difficulties for approximately eighteen months, and finally, someone could see me, hear me, and understand me. For so long, when talking about these difficulties, others would wonder if perhaps I may have been that way in the past and I just hadn't noticed. Others would comment saying how well I was doing or highlighted the positives. While I was also someone who focused on the positives, I appreciated the acknowledgement; it felt so good to have someone validate these difficulties, for once, and say that it was actually a thing. I was even able to tolerate the word 'stroke' being used, something I had been struggling with saying myself or hearing other people say about me. Up until now, I hadn't felt that the word 'stroke' described my illness. To me, a 'stroke' seemed a broad term which included three different types of strokes. Using the word just didn't seem to fit for me. From my perspective, I needed to clarify what had happened which was a subarachnoid haemorrhage or brain haemorrhage, so I tended to just stick to the latter. Something about 'stroke' had an association with an older population and a somewhat serious condition, and I just wasn't ready to go there emotionally.

An appointment with the Endocrinology Department followed soon after. Upon explaining my recent brain injury history and my concern with the pattern of thoughts and feelings possibly linked to my hormones, the registrar reported that he needed to discuss this with the consultant and left the room. The Consultant Endocrinologist appeared in the office and took a seat, with the registrar standing to her side. The consultant announced that I had a condition called premenstrual dysphoric disorder (PMDD).

"What is that?" I asked. The consultant informed me that it was a condition associated with the menstrual cycle and listed some of the symptoms: insomnia, mood swings, anxiety, depression, and difficulty in concentrating, among others. In listing the symptoms, I noted these overlapped with the symptoms of an acquired brain injury and I felt annoyed that PMDD was the instant conclusion drawn. I stated again the neuropsychologist had recommended the appointment for the investigation of a brain chemistry or hormone imbalance. Immediately, the consultant asked the location of the aneurysm in my brain.

Feeling my head tilt to the side, wondering where this was going, I replied, "The left communicating artery." She disparagingly replied that the part of the brain that controls emotions is the prefrontal cortex, and as the aneurysm was not at that part of the brain, it was PMDD and not brain injury related. "Wow, really," I thought sarcastically. How disappointing and incredibly frustrating this very brief interaction was. I did not feel the urge to reply or inform her that I was a psychologist myself with full awareness of the parts of the brain that controls emotions. I asked what the possible treatments were and she informed me that I could be prescribed an anti-depressant. Deep breath required and a pause taken. Possibly noting my desist, the consultant asked me how I felt about being prescribed medication.

"Like I want to run a million miles away from you," I replied, half in jest and whole in earnest. I was exasperated with this process. How deflating that the only course of action was to take medication. I told her I was a resourceful person and would prefer to observe, monitor, and track the situation, implementing my own methods of coping first before considering this route. It's not that I don't see a need for medication. Medication has its place and supports many to be well and stay well. For me, in this instance, there seemed to be a mismatch and it was not the best fit for me. Nonetheless, it was an avenue that was suggested, and with this new lens, I observed and monitored as time passed and supported myself where necessary, not allowing my thoughts and feelings to become too overwhelming, engaging in self-care practices and reaching out to chat to friends and family, not disconnecting more.

With COVID-19 restrictions and outpatient appointments on hold, the next MRI scan appointment was delayed. The hospital outsourced the appointment to a nearby clinic. However, the clinic would not accept me as a patient eligible for scanning due to the type of platinum coils in situ. The clinic requested the coil name and number so they could verify if their MRI machine was safe for me to be scanned in. In requesting this information from the hospital, the hospital decided that they would scan me there instead. But this set off some interesting and wild thoughts in my head. I had also just been watching a Netflix show, 'Black Mirror,' where, in the last episode, hacked robotic bees attacked targets by flying up their nose to short-circuit the victim's brain. For one victim, this painful experience resulted in a scan in hospital. As the scan machine started, the robotic bee was instantly magnetised to the scanner and propelled through the victim's eye. I wondered if the coils in my head could be affected in any way by anything in the environment. If a nearby clinic was refusing to scan me, what might that mean in the future? Shrugging it off, I assured myself that the hospital would have told me of any potential risks. With some time off work on the day of the appointment, I met my friend, Ashika, for lunch. In chatting, she asked if I was nervous or worried about the appointment. I reported that I wasn't feeling too bothered by the procedure as I was familiar with the process, and I was confident that I could stay calm and relaxed during it. It was more the worry at the back of my mind that there could be a new aneurysm developed or a problem with the current site. I didn't see the point in worrying unnecessarily about something I couldn't control. On the drive over to the hospital, driving behind a white van on the motorway, I got an unsettled, eery feeling. I was not sure why I was feeling this way, I wasn't worried in any way about the appointment. This feeling developed to being about the van in front of me, pressing on the brake pedal, I pulled back away from it. In a split second, smoke came from the van and the van veered over to the left part the lane and swayed back again as if losing control. Next, the tyre blew off the wheel and flew onto the road right in my path. I had no choice but to drive over it, as I couldn't get out of its way. Luckily, this all felt like it was happening in slow motion, and I managed to slow down and put my hazards on as a warning to the drivers behind. The van driver managed to cut across three lanes to the safety of the hard shoulder lane. I felt sick. "That could have been worse," I said to myself. But I was shaken. By the time I got to the car park of the hospital, parked, and walked to the radiology department, I had calmed my system down. I completed the necessary forms required and the radiologist briefly chatted with me about the clinic refusal. I questioned if I should be concerned about this and she reported that I had nothing to worry about. It was the clinic's precautionary attitude rather than any potential issue or risk. Taking a deep breath, I settled. The radiologist glanced over the form and asked if there were any new medical issues since I was last there. In replying there wasn't, she ushered me to the MRI table. Once I was all set, she placed the call buzzer in my hand and urged me to press it if I needed anything. As I entered the tunnel, suddenly a thought popped into my head, "I did have a change to my medical history since last time." Sheer panic set in. With my heart beating out of my chest, my body rigid with fear, and racing thoughts, screaming in my mind, "I now have new teeth," "I know I saw questions about dentures, but I didn't think about my new teeth," "What if there is some metal on them and I didn't tell the radiologist?" "Press the buzzer, press the buzzer now," "Will my teeth be pulled from my head just like the robotic bees?" Images flashed into my mind about the robotic bee, being replaced with my teeth. I could see teeth flying out, stuck to the machine wall. "What am I going to do?" "I need to get out," "I need to stop the machine," "Press the buzzer, press the buzzer," "The next sequence in the scan could be the one that does the damage." I knew this was completely irrational. I knew I had allowed myself to be taken off on this mad journey of pure terror. There was no logic to it. I began challenging those thoughts, asking, "Do you really believe this?" "Would the teeth not already be gone at this point?" "Your imagination is wild," "Nothing is going to happen," "Calm down," "I am safe," "Everything is going to be okay." I told myself to take a deep breath, and instantly, the rigid muscles of my body began to relax. I took some slow deep breaths, released the tight grip of the buzzer and was able to manage the rest of the scan. I met a friend after the scan and told him of my terror rollercoaster experience in my mind.

He laughed out loud, saying, "You watch too much TV!" Having worked in hospitals himself, he explained that my teeth would have launched towards the machine as soon as I walked in if it was going to happen. But not only that, the rooms have preventative measures in place to detect if there is metal present before entering the room.

"I wish I'd known that before the scan," I replied. How did I allow myself to get to that state? Nevertheless, I had talked myself down and was able to laugh at the places in my mind my thoughts took me.

After the first lockdown, in getting back to the gym, I was in good shape and feeling great in my body. But between another lockdown, working from home, and experiencing a new management style, let's name it micromanagement, I started to feel anxious again in my working life, which was spilling over into my personal life. For me, feeling tired, irritable, and edgy is all connected to anxiety. It is how it seems to manifest for me. Stronger feelings about having to prove myself to a new manager, coupled with the new manager's own anxiety in managing someone with a 'brain injury,' and my anxiety was through the roof. For the next couple of months of my life, I was faced with the constant reminder of my 'brain injury' and what I could not do.

With this style of management, I was making small mistakes more frequently, which always seemed to circle back to my brain injury. The more I tried to pre-empt my mistakes, the more mistakes I seemed to make. They were silly mistakes, things like writing something wrongly or ticking the wrong box on something. But I felt like I was failing in my work life, wondering if I would ever be good enough again. It became so difficult that I contemplated a career change. How was I here? Was this not the dream job? How am I still not happy with what was supposed to be my dream job? With an overall feeling of 'meh' in my personal life, COVID-19 and lockdown restrictions had a lot to answer for. It was Ashika who forwarded me an article on lockdown and the association of languishing. 'Languishing,' was the word I was looking for. That described how I was feeling completely. The New York Times article written by Adam Grant described languishing as the void between depression and flourishing and research highlighted that healthcare workers who were languishing in Spring 2020 were three times more likely to be diagnosed with post-traumatic stress disorder. The verb 'to languish' is defined as "being forced to remain in an unpleasant place or situation" or "to lose or lack vitality; grow weak."

It was no wonder I ended up with an asthma flare-up which required two doses of steroids and two weeks' sick leave. Between sounding like I smoked twenty-a-day and needing to rest after taking ten steps to go to the bathroom, I decided enough was enough. I needed to take back control of things in my life, one of them being my ability to breathe. As I scrolled through personal emails, I stumbled upon an email advertising the Wim Hof method.

I had heard of the 'Iceman' before this and was in admiration of his experimentations. But I hadn't given much thought to trying it out. When I investigated it, I realised it was quite accessible from home. In following his breathing guidance coupled with cold showers, I was well on my way to getting a handle on this breathing of mine. Encouraged by Dean, I even ventured out to join a large group to meditate and take a dip in the sea at moonlight on a cold winter's evening. The exhilaration I felt with that experience was immense. I felt alive and part of a collective. I then began going for a dip in the sea on a weekly basis. I noticed it was impacting positively on my training sessions as I was able to get more oxygen into my body. My breathing became coordinated with my movement. I started to recover and calm more quickly and I wasn't as panicked as before when my heart rate increased. Although this did not last long as another lockdown was disappointingly implemented. And so, back to languishing…

Chapter Thirteen

Anxiety

Are you starting to see the pattern with me here throughout this book? I have had opportunities in my younger life and not taken them up in the mode of my true self; my calm and relaxed self. That has primarily been down to anxiety and stress and allowing that state, unknowingly, to take over. Yes, any performer be it a sportsperson, stage performer or other, will tell you that, before an event, they all have a little of the anxious or nervous feelings I have described in the scenarios so far. The difference here is that some of that feeling aids optimal performance while too much of that feeling can be unproductive, destructive, and completely debilitating.

If we look at stress, what we know about stress is that, "Stress is a specific response the body makes to all non-specific demands… no matter what the situation is, when the demand we perceive exceeds the resources we think we have, the body and mind are aroused and geared up either to fight the change or flee from the situation to avoid harm." (Patel, 1996). Stress is also a negative emotional experience accompanied by predictable biochemical, physiological, cognitive, and behavioural changes that are directed either toward altering the stressful event or accommodating its effects (Taylor, 1998). According to Cannon, (1932) when we perceive that we are in danger, the primitive response mechanism is activated. This is the fight or flight response, to stay and fight or to run away (Ogden, 2007). The best-known biological theory is that of Hans Seyle called the General Adaptation Syndrome (GAS). He suggested that our bodies constantly strive to maintain a stable and consistent state called homeostasis and the body attempts to restore this homeostasis by means of an adaptive response. This theory consists of three stages: alarm reaction, resistance, and exhaustion. During the first stage—alarm reaction, is when a stressor first occurs. The body responds to the perceived danger with a physiological response to the stress: the fight, flight, fright or fawn stage.

Chemicals are released: cortisol and adrenaline. These aid with speeding up the heart rate to pump more oxygen in the blood around the body to the muscles and vital organs. Our breathing quickens to accommodate this. The pupils dilate to allow light in to best see what we are doing. Our muscles become tense, geared up and ready. We may experience butterflies in our stomach or a churning sensation. We may feel a tightening in our chest, fast breathing, sweaty palms, sweaty in general, overheated, headache, and dry mouth, among other symptoms. The digestive system slows down or stops as the body focuses on sending the energy to survive the perceived threat. This is the body gearing up to stay and 'fight,' often becoming aggressive or to flee or 'flight,' run away from a situation. 'Fright' is where the body freezes, incapable of moving or decision-making and 'fawn' is the response to moving to accommodate the other person or to people-please to avoid any conflict.

If stage one is prolonged, then stage two is set in motion, resistance. Resistance is where the body tries to sustain homeostasis and there is then a sensitivity to stress. If an elevated level of stress continues then stage three is reached, the stage of exhaustion. At this stage, the body can no longer resist the original stressor and an affective experience can occur such as anxiety and depression (Seyle, 1956). Professor Paul Gilbert, Consultant Clinical Psychologist, refers to the threat detection system in compassion focused therapy (CFT). This is activated by physical threat, emotional threat, and social threat. The function of this system is to alert our attention to danger or threat and gear us towards survival and safety.

During my mid-twenties, I attended a workplace training called 'Address that Stress' with my one-and-only mother, Regina, delivering the course. Some of the above information was relayed with suggestions of ways to manage stress. The first step is always the state of awareness, to be able to identify what stress means for you in your body. What clues does your body give you that tell you that you are stressed? Then, the next step is knowing what to do. It was here that I realised what had happened to me those couple of years previous, as a teenager. I was not able to defend myself, never mind fight back that time on the way home from school, because it was a physiological response to stress that I seemed to default to, 'fright-mode.' Fright-mode and flight-mode tended to be my defaults. All that time I had spent talking negatively to myself, expecting myself to be able to do better, and I couldn't, due to an automatic response, a trauma response.

During my undergraduate study in psychology, a large part of the course involved studying psychoanalysis. It was during a module on Freudian case histories, that I became rather rattled by one case history in particular, The Ratman. The Ratman was a case involving a man who had an obsessive fear of something happening to his father, involving the rat punishment. This punishment involved a large vessel containing a live rat, strapped to the buttocks of the victim, and the rat, encouraged by a red-hot poker, would gnaw its way out through the victim's anus. I can usually conjure good visual imagery in my mind and I found this case disturbing. I already had an experience of mice scurrying in the walls of the first house I lived in after I moved out of home, and that was enough to induce a fear, never mind thinking about the rat punishment. But it is true; what we think about, focus on, and give our energy to, can become our reality. Subsequently, at that time, over the Christmas holiday period, a rat had found its way into the utility area in my place of work. It had been caught in a trap, but even still, this triggered real fear in me. It got to the point where the threat system was constantly activated, I was on high alert all the time, worrying about rats scurrying around. One dark winter night walking from college to the car park in Dublin City Centre, I caught sight of something in my peripheral vision rustling down the other side of the street. This triggered me to react and skedaddle out of there. It turned out it was only an empty crisp packet that sent me running down the street in sheer panic! A full-on physiological response as if a lion were chasing me and I was running for my life. I thought, enough is enough, I need to get this sorted. My body was 'switching on' at a significant rate and I didn't seem able to 'switch off' or calm myself at all. I was edgy, nervy, and tense. I knew I needed a therapy, possibly a cognitive behavioural therapy (CBT) of some sort, and I went about researching reputable professionals. This is where I met the late Dr David Carey, a kind, gentle and 'honey-toned' man. He was an American psychologist who I understood to be a counselling psychologist at the time. He had ample respect for early years educators in general, referring to the American perspective of preschool as being quite different, more progressive, than that of Ireland at that current time. I found this extremely refreshing and I felt immensely respected. I had numerous therapy sessions with him, and in discussing the incidences of bullying in my teenage years, I got talking about how I believed all the analysing or over-analysing of the different ways around managing to get to and from school and home safely or trying to work out every eventuality, I had developed skills of being able to see problems from many different angles. Imagining myself in the other person's shoes in what they might be thinking or how they might attack had allowed me to see other people's perspectives and develop strategic planning, somewhat. Dr David Carey reported how remarkable I was at being able to change such an adverse experience into a positive outcome. He said that he would have loved me to be able to speak to a young client of his who was experiencing a similar experience to that of mine and how wonderfully empowering it would be for them to see me, where I was at some ten years or so on from my experience. I found his feedback encouraging.

CBT and talk therapy had a positive outcome for me in this instance, restoring my body's sense of calm and relieving the fear of rats entering my workplace or anywhere else for that matter! I believe there are many successful therapy modalities and there is not a one-size-fits-all, there can't be. But different modalities are called for at various times. Some many years later, I encountered Dr David Carey as a guest lecturer in my Educational Psychology training course. When I saw his name come up on a list of books for recommended reading and a list of lecturers, I was in awe at his work in advocating and supporting children with additional needs. I remember feeling nervous about seeing him again and how appropriate it might be. My class was a small class size of only seventeen, and when discussing the key role of early years educators in young children's education and development, he looked and me and winked, and I felt proud of the conversation we had previously and was put at complete ease. After the lectures, he stopped me outside the building briefly. He stated that it was good to see me and how delighted he was to see I was on the programme. He shook my hand and wished me all the best in my career, stating, he believed I would make a wonderful psychologist. I shyly thanked him but was secretly beaming. I had written him a short letter after our therapy sessions had finished, thanking him for his help and support but I don't think he really had any idea of the impact he had on me, both from a therapeutic perspective and as a role model for my future psychology career.

Another example of 'fright mode' is when I volunteered for a helpline for children. I volunteered weekly for two years. What I noticed upon the initial training was how shy I was and how I did not like the spotlight of doing role play or answering in the larger group. I would get nervous and feel anxious in the large group and I would relax as soon as the role play was over, or the focus was off having to perform in some way. When it came to taking live calls, despite ten days of intensive training, I went into fright mode. I could not think of what to say. My brain went completely blank, I could not word find or put a sentence together. Being on the phone really highlighted how much non-verbal communication I tended to rely on by gesturing, raising my eyebrows, nodding, or shaking my head. Luckily, I had a buddy in place to prompt and support me. From that first call, I made a script for myself and practised it. It soon became automatic and I did not need that script any more. I was feeling confident with my ability to manage the call and I was delighted with the feedback from my supervisor about having a lovely natural tone on the calls, which was something she said cannot be trained. But I was still struggling, with one type of call in particular. It was especially noticeable, to me, on a call to a group of girls. That seemed to activate me, reminding me of the teenage bullying by a group of girls. It involved some work to develop coping skills for those calls. With the support of my supervisor, I managed to, and my confidence grew.

During my time as an early years educator and commensurate with the helpline work, I trained in the HighScope Preschool Implementation programme, a preschool curriculum programme devised by an American psychologist, Dr David Weikart. It contained a conflict resolution technique for children and I found I loved this process. It worked extremely well. But it also gave me a framework to work from in managing my own conflicts and supported me with additional skills for my own interpersonal relationships.

A few years later, while dabbling with some yoga, the yoga teacher put out an invitation from a student of a positive psychology course looking for volunteers to participate in some research. This student offered four sessions in positive psychology as part of her research, and I decided to sign up to see what it was all about. It was interesting and built on some practices I already knew. She briefly introduced me to the idea of mindfulness and a representational system: V.A.K.G.O. or using the five senses; visualisation, auditory, kinaesthetic, gustatory, and olfactory. I was asked to access memories from the best times in my life and connect in with remembering the event using the five senses. Having practised that, she then encouraged me to imagine a future goal achieved, she got me to practice it already happening or achieved using V.A.K.G.O. I found this practice extremely helpful. This practice then seemed to be a primer for a plethora of work with Derry McDermott using the influences of Abraham-Hicks and the emotional scale, among other modalities. It was here where Derry supported me to work towards gaining many of my life achievements: passing my driving test, gaining my degree in psychology, purchasing property, enabling me to leave social housing, gaining entry to the Educational Psychology Masters programme after two failed attempts, and gaining my master's degree. I always walked into those sessions with one agenda and walked away acquiring so much more insight about myself or the situation. The work always ended up being about the feeling in the body; shifting my vibration to that of a higher feeling vibration than when I had walked in.

Play was also a big part of my life every day when I worked in preschool. When my children were younger, I also had the opportunity to play on the weekends, when I wasn't working. What I noticed during my psychologist training was the transition from being with children every day to being with adults all day every day. I noticed my mood was lower. Self-doubt, feeling anxious and imposter syndrome also featured heavily during my first year. No offence to adults but children are much more fun, especially three-, four- and five-year-olds. They're so open, honest and carefree and it is glorious to match them on that vibrational level. It keeps you young! Sometimes I forgot I was an adult and became five-years-old again when I played, honoured that the children allowed me into their play.

It took me time to realise that I was missing this play in my life but studying and achieving my goal was enough of a distraction. My dream to work as a psychologist finally came, was finally achieved. But working with children as a psychologist can be quite different from working or being at play with children. It has a much more clinical vibe to it. It must, by the very nature of it. Post training and in my first job, the job was much more of an 'office job' than I had expected. With the loss of this 'play' in my life, I think, in some ways, I was seeking things to replicate that loss of play. I believe as adults we must find that 'play,' those fun activities we like doing that make us laugh and keep us young, whatever that looks like for each one of us. I found I was exploring that side much more. With a full-time course completed and no study distractions, I had so much free time on my hands. Seeking out fun or 'play' was what I needed to do to combat any stress in my life.

Feeling like we have the skills, tools, and support to be able to manage anything that life throws at us is John Mayer's definition of resilience. Feeling like 'a fish in water' aligns with a sense of identity and a sense of belonging and is one way to counteract stress and anxiety.

All too often when we feel like we don't know what we are doing or how to handle something, our bodies perceive we are in danger and 'switch on'. This can lead to us experiencing overwhelming feelings of dread as we cannot find solutions to problems we are not even sure exist yet, projecting into the future with all the 'what ifs?'. All too often that is not fun and we find we are on the road to misery.

Chapter Fourteen

Changes

Having described my story so far, you can see why my wellness needs to be a priority in my life. I do not want illness to be my focus. Some people differ slightly in their theory or idea of wellness or well-being, but according to the World Health Organisation, 'well-being' is a "resource for healthy living" and a "positive state of health" that is "more than the absence of an illness" and enables us to function well: psychologically, physically, emotionally, and socially.

As wellness can differ for everyone, wellness to me is:

1. Healthy food or nutrition, a healthy balanced diet
2. Adequate, quality sleep
3. Exercise, physical movement
4. Social engagement and good relationships
5. Spiritual
6. Emotional

This chapter is not about addressing 'wellness' overall, with me, suggesting that I have expertise in all areas of wellness. It is, of course, about balance rather than going all out to extremes in one or two of the areas above. I am still on a journey of recovery and discovery about myself; who I am now post-illness, what my needs are and how I best meet those needs. This is, in fact, a balancing act and one I have yet to master.

Like most people, I have to work at keeping a 'good enough' diet. I don't eat certain foods, mainly based on my preferences, but also based on the impact certain foods have on my body. I have a gluten sensitivity rather than an intolerance altogether, so I tend to monitor that. Being asthmatic, I have reduced dairy in my diet as, according to myth rather than science, dairy products tend to build mucus in the lungs. Chocolate, particularly, is my nemesis so, if I can keep that to a minimum, I am doing well. I try to stick to the eighty/twenty principle. I've tried numerous diets over the years and they have resulted in weight loss, but none are as sustainable as the eighty/twenty principle. I want to be able to enjoy my life. Life is for living. I don't want to be miserable trying to stick to low calories or the complete avoidance of certain foods.

As a psychologist, I know good quality sleep is important. Since insomnia was a symptom after brain injury and knowing how it did and still can impact on my daily functioning, I have to ensure good sleep patterns and good sleep hygiene:

•Going to bed at the same time each night.
•Waking up at the same time each morning.

•Making sure my bedroom is relaxing, a comfortable temperature, and quiet.

•Not watching TV or having electronics in my bedroom.

•Managing my worries or anxious feelings before getting into bed.

Still, with all the above in place, when I'm stressed, my sleep can be affected considerably. Not being able to relax enough to fall asleep easily. Even when I do fall asleep, I can be restless and then I find getting up in the morning difficult. At one point during lockdown, I was struggling badly to fall asleep. I was staying up later than I should have as a way to rebel, I think. In this way, I had control over something during such a restricted time. But in the end, I was only hurting myself. I was getting approximately four hours of sleep per night. Now, for some, they may think four hours is not too bad. But not for me. I was always someone who needed eight hours minimum to function. Even as a baby, I used to fall asleep sitting up in my highchair after dinner. That was just who I was. But even more now, after the illness, I need extra sleep. I have always found meditation or guided meditation helpful at bedtime, but I can fall in and out of habit with it. Now, I find connecting in with the moment, the best way to help me fall asleep once all the above is in place. Deactivating any negative emotions is also helpful. Then listening and focusing in on the environment sounds, coupled with some positive thoughts, "I am calm, I am relaxed, I am safe, permission to sleep," and I can fall asleep more easily and quickly.

Exercise is a big part of my life. As I mentioned earlier, sports, particularly football, featured heavily in my younger life and got me through some tough teenage years. So, it is only fitting that exercise still features heavily in my life now. It was my main motivator in getting back to health. In some ways, exercise is my body's meditation. My body feels so good after exercise and I can have such clarity of thought or great ideas can come to me during or after exercise. The changes that I have taken note of are the frequency and type of exercise I engage in. I love having a variety of exercise in my life. But I have to manage my fatigue. This means not being tempted to go to the gym twice a day like in the past. Or using exercise to escape or numb my feelings. Now, it is more about building in rest days and restorative activity like walking.

Social engagement and good relationships are about a sense of belonging to a community and making a contribution to society. Becoming ill helped to remind me who was important in my life. The important people showed up for me and the ones who did not, do not feature heavily in my life. A good friend, Karla, helped me to look at social contracting and the impact that can have on my life. A social contract is when we have a set of rules, expectations, and boundaries that define that relationship. The meaningful exchanges we have within our relationships will vary depending on the type of relationship. For example, our relationship with a spouse will look different to that of a friend or colleague or stranger. Looking at my relationships in that way and becoming more aware, helped me in making decisions about people who may have been impacting my life in a negative way. For example, we might find we have a relationship in our lives that takes the form of a more transactional and often one-way interaction and we need to decide if we are to continue in this way with this person. It can be tricky to see people in that light. But the suggestion would be to keep interactions with those who may be deemed more toxic to us to a minimum. Having good boundaries helps. On a more positive note, the relationships that help resource you, that fill you up, that are fun, meaningful, and engaging are the ones you want in your life. So, keep those up!

Spiritual well-being can include feeling connected to a higher power, a sense of meaning or purpose or feelings of peace or transcendence. I believe I have found that connection. I have found source energy. I have seen it in my near-death experience. I have intuitive wisdom. I just need to keep stress at bay to hear it! Spirituality can be an individual practice often relating to the process of developing beliefs relating to the meaning of life and the connectedness to others. This might take the form of different terminology for different people and whatever our beliefs in connectedness, however they may differ or, in fact, be the same, is okay.

In looking at Plato's theory of forms, ultimate reality exists beyond our physical world, most famously discussed in The Republic. Plato suggests that there are two realms: the physical realm and the spiritual realm or non-physical realm. The physical realm is the material things we see and interact with daily, this physical state. The spiritual realm or non-physical realm has independently existing abstract perfect ideas or forms and does not exist in any time or space. For example, these ideas or forms are often explained as a perfect geometric shape such as a triangle. According to Plato, for any conceivable thing or property, there is a corresponding form, a perfect example of that thing or property in the non-physical realm (David Macintosh 2012). In applying this to me, and in my interpretation, there is a comfort in my near-death experience. Seeing the energy and the glimpse of opportunity to return to a non-physical realm, I am calm in the belief that I am now free to live my life. I do not need to strive for perfection. For there is already the perfect form of me (whatever that may be) in the non-physical realm. That is not to say that I don't have standards for myself or that I am not enthusiastic about what I do. It just now allows me to be calmer and more relaxed as I go about my days.

Emotional well-being means feeling good. Being happy, experiencing positive emotions like love, joy, or compassion, and feeling generally satisfied with life. Research also shows that people who report higher levels of well-being tend to be more likely to recover quicker from a range of chronic diseases. Winnicott, a Child Psychoanalyst, coined the term 'Good Enough Mother' in the 1950s. Since then, others have built on the concept terming it, 'Good Enough Parenting.' This is the idea that parents try their best to put their children's needs ahead of their own despite circumstances and what they can actually provide. In this sense, I have what I like to call, 'good enough wellness,' 'good enough fitness,' and 'good enough nutrition.' With wellness, for me, as I said, balance is key. Making sure I have a balanced approach in each of the areas of my life despite circumstances and what I can actually provide. Tip the scale to focusing extremely on one area and you can be knocked off-balance. On the other hand, if there is an area of your life that needs more work or more focus to bring it up to the level of all the other areas, then certainly, yes, more sustained focus is needed there, until there is some synchronicity. Take my recovery as an example. It was easier to focus on my physical side. Working hard to restore my physical fitness seemed tangible, with goal setting and marked evidence when those goals were achieved. With the cognitive side, being a psychologist, I knew my areas of weakness, it was glaringly obvious to me. Attention and concentration, auditory memory, brain fog and brain fatigue were the primary areas of weakness, and although this was a sore point, I could see improvements all the time. My emotional side, however, was somewhat different. I lost a lot of skills that I had developed or was still developing to support myself emotionally. I lost composure and confidence when it came to emotional control. It was harder to set goals and to see those being achieved. The trauma of the event itself still needed to be processed and that doesn't just happen overnight or with the wave of a magic wand. Never mind having to rebuild the skills that were already there at one point in time. Skilled professional support is key to this. Knowing that you need help and seeking the correct support is important. Having people who understand, who get you and who may have expertise in a particular condition, such as brain injury, can be very supportive.

Self-care must also be a priority. For me, I have to pace myself; I have to look after myself. I have to mind that. Having hobbies and interests or meeting up with family and friends that drain your battery is not good. Having hobbies and interests and good relationships that fill the battery is what you need. Rest and reflection are also needed. I think there will be periods in our lives when we can accomplish more by doing less because we are balancing our schedule which leaves us feeling energetic and enthusiastic rather than physically exhausted and mentally drained.

Our activities also need to include a soothing element. I mentioned Professor Paul Gilbert, Clinical Psychologist, earlier when describing the threat system. The system that detects and alerts us to danger. He suggests we have three systems: the threat system, the drive system, and the soothe system. The drive system motivates us and encourages us to seek out resources for ourselves and others. This system is about striving, achieving, and consuming and just as the threat system is basic for our survival, the drive system is also basic to our survival as it supports us to be resourceful in searching out food, to be ambitious with work, gain qualifications, and achieve. The emotions involved in this system are excitement, joy, and anticipation. We can feel energised as the hormone released in this system is dopamine, the reward hormone. Out of balance though, and this can lead people to pursue and achieve things in unhealthy ways. For example, with stress, perfectionism, burn out and addiction. The soothe system involves feeling soothed, at peace, connected to others and content. Feeling peaceful, relaxed, and playful occurs as the hormone oxytocin is released. It helps us to slow down and be calm. This system is less important for short-term survival but what is needed for long-term survival. Adverse experiences can lead people to have difficulty activating the soothe system. Some soothing exercises involve soothing rhythm breathing, walking in nature, meditation, and playing with a pet, for example.

In applying this theory to my own life; directly before my illness, I was operating between the threat and drive systems. I thought I was engaging in elements of the soothe system, as I was engaging in holistic therapies, meditation and what I deemed healthy activity. However, the drive and motivation to set goals and reach targets in my health far outweighed anything I was doing in the soothe system. For example, with the gym. I was pushing myself and being hard on myself with weight loss and fitness goals. The dopamine release and rewards from the gym high only motivated me to continue to strive for that 'high' again. Even though I was engaging in a healthy physical activity, I wasn't talking very nicely to myself, scrutinising my body shape, and pushing harder to achieve. I was also feeling extremely guilty about the indecision to stay or leave my marriage and I wasn't talking very nicely to myself about that either. When the self-critic is activated, this activates the threat system, releasing adrenaline, leading to feelings of fear and anxiety. I wasn't connecting in with what my body was really feeling and the gym high, among other aspects, allowed me to be distracted from the emotional pain my body was feeling. My body was flooded with adrenaline and dopamine hormones and couldn't seem to get off the fast-paced hamster wheel I found myself on.

We can activate the soothe system by being kind to ourselves. To do this, we talk to ourselves as we would talk to someone else. Reducing self-criticism and not being so hard on ourselves helps our brain and body. Self-criticism stimulates the stress response in the body. Therefore, the higher the levels of self-criticism, the higher the levels of stress, activating the threat system. Research by Paul Gilbert using the CFT model shows smiling to ourselves as we talk kindly in soothing tones has a significant positive impact.

I am now engaging in compassionate self-correction, by embracing my mistakes. During a recent session with the Neuropsychologist, Elaine, I discovered this has unfolded very naturally in the past eight months or so. So, what had changed in the nearly two years since last speaking to her? Her recommendation had been to engage more in self-compassion. But I hadn't really implemented that. Instead, in the first year since speaking to the Neuropsychologist, the micromanagement style of leadership and the spotlight on 'brain injury' had sparked a platform for anxiety and self-doubt to multiply. So, the soothe system was not being activated. In fact, it was back to the sway of threat to drive, drive to threat again. That was why I was feeling like I was back to languishing and questioning what I was doing in my career.

In starting a new job with a new line manager and a new senior clinical supervisor, the new line manager and supervisor both use a style of management, leadership, and supervision really conducive to my health. They have shifted the culture of error and punishment, modelling how human it is to make mistakes, and by modelling compassion. Shortly after beginning my new job, I had a call with international best-selling author, Mick Petersen. I attended a masterclass hosted by Peggy McColl, New York Times best-selling author, for authors or people interested in writing a book. Mick told his story at the masterclass of how he became the author of the book, 'Stella and the Timekeepers,' and how he has gone on to write more books and programmes. Intrigued by his story, I organised a call with him. Not only did his story and his charisma inspire me to continue my writing journey, but something he highlighted on that call reactivated a forgotten practice. He told me a clever way to check in with my thoughts is to give the negative thoughts a character with a name. When checking in or challenging my thoughts, I can then ask the character if it is their thought or my thought.

"Interesting... I'm going to give that a go." I said. I decided since gremlins had featured in my life already, referring my negative thoughts to gremlins in the past, likening my foraging for chocolate to that of a gremlin, and the gremlin's visit in hospital, I would call my character after the evilest gremlin, 'Stripe.' From there, every time I had a negative thought, I paused, and asked, "Is that you Stripe?" If it was not my thought or belief, I then said, "Stripe, out, you can leave," and it worked!

Since then and in the brief time in my new job, I have shifted from a focus of believing that my mistakes stem from that of brain injury, to mistakes being a natural human experience, and as such, my mistakes are more infrequent, and if any happen, it is not a big deal now. I began to activate my soothe system by talking kindlier to myself with a smile. I feel like I can do my job now. I am trusted. I feel like I can breathe. How joyous to feel something as fundamental as the ability to breathe and yet the significance of this is profound. I have a restored and recovered tool in the 'breath', life's golden secret. Something we take for granted in life. Something we often don't show appreciation or gratitude for. An autonomic bodily function we don't have to think about. But by thinking about the breath, by gaining an awareness and control of my breathing, along with checking my thoughts, and saying kind words to myself, helps me to stay in control of my emotions, and in turn, helps me to produce ideas to problem solve efficiently and be creative.

I recently found an old audio recording on my phone of a singing lesson. I can hear the stress in my voice. The stress is almost palpable with each ascending note. As I reflect on that time now, I'm unsure as to what I was so worried about. Really, the worst that could have happened was that I noticed I couldn't sing higher than the last note, that I'd reached my top range. In following along with the recording now, what I notice is the ease in which I allow the breath to come and go. It feels so nice now to understand the process of breathing for singing. In singing along now with the old audio recording, it feels so good, so easy, and much better than before.

I don't think anything I am saying here in this chapter is new or unique. What I am saying is that I have been through an experience that has shown me a different way to live my life, a way of being. A way that I was working towards but somehow had lost my way, along the way. What I am aware of now, is to enjoy the unfolding, for the unfolding is the journey of life. It can be so hurried in our day-to-day life that we miss life itself. The unfolding is the enjoyment that comes in experiencing the moment. The joy of noticing. Noticing our surroundings, noticing nature, noticing our thoughts, noticing our feelings, noticing our relationships, and noticing our children. Don't get distracted by technology; phones, social media, and the likes for our media lives, is scrolling endlessly, passing the time. Instead, listen to the birds' tweets, listen to the trees whisper as they sway in the breeze, listen to the rainfall. Listen to the traffic, the hustle and bustle. It all brings us to awareness. To be present in our minds can be difficult if it is cluttered with negative thoughts. Pay attention to those thoughts. Check in that those thoughts are our own thoughts and not a by-product of somebody else's conditioning, someone else's energy of words taken on by our minds. Check-in with our own body to become aware of the feeling or the sensation it is telling us. Live from the inside out. So many of us are consumed by external influences to help what we perceive will 'make' us happy: consumables, material items, relationships, courses of study and unhealthy behaviours. With the idea of 'when I have this, then I will be happy.' 'When I have my new car, then I will be happy,' 'When I have more money, then I will be happy,' 'When I get a promotion, then I will be happier,' or 'Being with this person, will make me happier.' The 'being happy' has to come from within. We have to be happy within ourselves before we can be happy in a relationship. The external items: the car, a holiday, clothes, or any other item, isn't going to make us happy. Certainly, a holiday, a rest to recover and rejuvenate is well-needed and will support wellness. Certainly, having a new car feels good, it can feel amazing. Certainly, a new handbag, piece of jewellery or any other item can also feel good. However, this can be short-lived, a short-term sensation before the need to seek externally begins again. But those external items don't 'make' you happy. Because you have to decide you want to be happy.

Because that is how you want to feel—to want to align with the high vibrational feelings, the connectedness of self.

Upon reflecting on my life for the past forty-two years, I'm aware that I have, according to Daniel Gilbert, an American psychologist, a 'psychological immune system' that shields me from the worst effects of any misfortune. Where I am right now, with an acquired brain injury, is that an acquired brain injury does not define me. Rather it informs me. I can now tell people I had a stroke. I am more able to accept what has happened to me and live in the present moment, not looking back at the awfulness of that event or the many others in my life. A part of my brain ruptured, rupturing my life, my relationships and who I was. It halted my life. But in the repair, was the opportunity to stop and reflect on my life and repair the most important relationship of all: the relationship I have with myself and how I chose to be happy. I decided that was how I wanted to be.

Life is for living now. Be excited to be alive. If we don't live in the present moment, either looking back remorsefully or looking to the future anxiously, worried about the next thing, then we lose sight of the now. We don't know what can happen in an instant to change our lives forever. So, be present, enjoy and be who you want to be.

To be continued…